Secret Plac

AVEYRON

Written & Researched
by
John Couth   R.J Snowden

Photographs
by
John Couth

Series Editor:
Robin Dewhurst

1st Edition
Includes Index
ISBN 0 9534537 0 7

Published by
Secret Place Publications
Head Office 1 Brooklands Avenue, Cleethorpes. DN35 8QP
secret.places@btinternet.com

Printed by
GSB, 32 Hainton Avenue, Grimsby DN35 9BB

Cover Design by	**Technical advice from**
Alan Bridges	James Jackaman & Martin Birkett

Layout by
S.J.Couth

First Publication
December1998

Although the authors and publishers have tried to make the information as accurate as possible, they accept no responsibility for any loss, injury or inconvenience sustained by any person using this book.

Text & Maps Copyrights
Secret Place Publications 1998

Photographs Copyright
John Couth 1998

All rights reserved. No part of this publication may be reproduced, stored in a retrieval system or transmitted in any form by any means, electronic, mechanical, photocopying, recording or otherwise, except brief extracts for the purpose of review, without the written permission of the publisher and copyright owner.

LANDSCAPE

The red earth is the blood in my veins,
The rocks are my bones, the grass my hair,
The hilltop, where I watch the days, my church,
The mountain my cathedral. The eagle, burning
The air, forging the four winds,
Is the One shadow, claws of my God descending,
Deliverer from this landscape of perpetual season.

Jacques Bâtides

Contents

Background — Part 1

- **HOW TO USE THE BOOK** — 8
- **AVEYRON** — 9
- **MAP OF AVEYRON** — 10
- **INTRODUCTION** - Living History, At A Glance History, Administrative Divisions, Villages, Houses, Farm Buildings, Chateaux, Bastides — 11
- **FOOD** - Les Fromages, Le Stockfish, La Fouace, Le Tripou, Les Truffes, Les Champignons, Les Noix, Les Canards and Les Oies — 21
- **LES VINS** - Marcillac, Entraygues et le Fel, Estaing, Vins des Gorges et Côtes de Millau — 31
- **USEFUL INFORMATION** - Tourism, Tourist Information, Getting There and Getting Around, Contacting by Telephone and Letter, Places To Stay, Eating Out — 35

The Guide Book — Part 2

- **THE NORTH** - Introduction — 51
- **Le Carladez-the far north** - Mur-de-Barrez, Thérondels, Brommat, Lacroix-Barrez — 54
- **From the Montagnes d'Aubrac to the Lakes and the Truyère** - Sainte-Geneviève-sur-Argence, Lacalm, Cassuéjouls, Laguiole, Saint-Chély-d'Aubrac and Aubrac, Castelnau-de-Mandailles, Saint-Amans-des-Cots and the Lakes, Le Nayrac, Saint-Symphorien-de-Thénières — 57
- **The Pays d'Olt (The Upper Lot Valley)** - Saint-Laurent-d'Olt, Saint-Geniez-d'Olt, Sainte-Eulalie-d'Olt, Saint-Côme-d'Olt, Espalion, Estaing, Golinhac, Entraygues-sur-Truyère, Enguialès — 65
- **Between Entraygues-sur-Truyère and Conques** - Sénergues and Esperac — 72
- **South and West of Conques** - Conques, Saint-Cyprien-sur-Dourdou, Auzits, Cransac, — 73

Aubin, Decazeville, Bouillac, Livinhac-le-Haut, Flagnac, Capdenac-Gare

Hotel and Camping Suggestions — 82

THE CENTRE - Introduction — 86
Villefranche-de-Rouergue — 90
North West of Villefranche-de-Rouergue - Savignac and Loc Dieu, Martiel, Sainte-Croix, Montsalès, Salvagnac-Cajarc, Ambeyrac, Balagier-d'Olt — 93
North East of Villefranche-de-Rouergue Villeneuve-d'Aveyron, Druhle and Peyrusse-le-Roc, Montbazens — 97
East of Villefranche-de-Rouergue - La Bastide-L'Evêque, Compolibat and Prévinquières, Belcastel, Bournazel — 100
Najac — 103
East of Najac - Monteils, Sanvensa, La Fouillade, Lunac and the Cheval de Roi, Saint-André-de-Najac and Lagard-Viaur(Tarn), Rieupeyroux, La Salvetat-Payralès, Pradinas, La Capelle-Bleys, Sauveterre-de-Rouergue, Naucelle, Camjac — 105
Rodez — 114
West of Rodez - Marcillac, Salles-la-Source, Muret-le-Château, Rodelle, Baraqueville — 117
East of Rodez - Bouzouls, Montrozier, Bertholène, Séverac-le-Château, The Causse de Séverac and the Serre Valley, Campagnac, Pierrefiche-d'Olt, The Northern Plateau du Lévezou, Vezins-de-Lévezou, Pont-de-Salars and the Lakes, Salles-Curan — 121

Hotel and Camping Suggestions — 128

THE SOUTH - Introduction — 133
Millau — 136
The Causse du Larzac and the *Circuit du Larzac Templier et Hospitalier* - La Couvertoirade, Saint-Jean-d'Alcas, Le Viala-du-Pas-de-Jaux, Sainte-Eulalie-de-Cernon, La Cavalerie, Nant, Saint-Jean-du-Bruel — 138
The Causse Noir and River Gorges - Paulhe, Aguessac, Compeyre, La Cresse, Rivière-sur-Tarn, — 143

Mostuéjouls, Peylereau, Le Causse Noir, Veyreau, Saint-André-de-Vezines, La Roque-Sainte-Marguerite, Saint-Véran

The Tarn Valley (West of Millau) - Compregnac, Saint-Rome-de-Tarn, Brousse-le-Château — 149

The Réquista Area - Réquista, Villefranche-de-Panat, Durenque, Alrance, Cassagnes-Bégonhès — 151

Plateau du Lévezou (North West of Millau) - Montjaux, Castelnau-Péygayrolles, Saint-Beauzely, Saint-Léons, Saint-Laurent-du-Lévezou — 154

North and East of Saint-Affrique - Saint-Affrique, Roquefort, Tournemire, La Bastide-Pradines, Saint-Rome-de-Cernon — 157

West of Saint-Affrique - Coupiac, Plaisance, La Bastide-Solages, Saint-Sernin-sur-Rance, Belmont-sur-Rance — 162

South and South East of Saint-Affrique - Montlaur, Camarès, Brusque — 164

Hotel and Camping Suggestions — 167

Glossary — 171

Reading — 173

Index — 175

The River Lot

Maps of the Region

Aveyron	10
The North	51
Le Carladez - the far North	54
The Montagnes d'Aubrac (Lakes & Truyere)	57
The Pays d'Olt	65
South and West of Conques	73
The Centre	86
North West of Villefranche-de-Rouergue	93
North East of Villefranche-de-Rouergue	97
East of Villefranche-de-Rouergue	100
East of Najac	105
West of Rodez	117
East of Rodez	121
Pont-de-Salars and the Lakes	126
The South	133
The Causse du Larzac	138
The Causse Noir and River Gorges	143
The Tarn Valley, West of Millau	149
The Requista Area	151
Plateau du Levezou	154
North and East of Saint Afrique	157
West of Saint Afrique	161
South and South East of Saint Afrique	164

Using the Book

The first part of the book, the Introduction, has been compiled to give you a general idea of the geography, history, archaeology and the amenities for tourism that exist in the department of Aveyron.

The second part, which is the guide to the cities, towns, villages and countryside of the region, divides the department up into three sections - the North, the Centre and the South. Within each section, smaller geographical areas are described, prefaced by a line-map and followed by a brief outline of the main places of interest.

> ~ Each of these smaller areas can be regarded as a day or half-day trip. Though you are more likely to centre your visit on a single place, like let's say Conques, in which case you can use the book to see what else might be worth visiting in the immediate area. Or you can use it further to select towns, villages, restaurants or picnic spots to visit en route to and from your destination.

> ~ The listed campsites, hotels and restaurants contained at the end of each of the sections are by no means comprehensive, nor should they be always taken as a guarantee of high quality. They have, however, been selected on the basis of personal experience and/or recommendation and form a representative sample in the main towns and sites of natural significance throughout the region.

A final point is that the book will be of most use in conjunction with a good map of Aveyron and, if you're walking or cycling, the relevant *Série Bleue* map which has every dwelling, lane and footpath clearly indicated.

AVEYRON

On Arrival

The gear shift is imperceptible, but slowly the landscape comes to enfold you. The roads lose their directness and grow to resemble the crayon scribblings of a child. The racetrack drivers of the autoroutes, who tailgate you in their underpowered cars, have slipped noisily away. And you have joined another sort of daredevil, closer to some low mountain stage of the *Tour de France* where instead of avoiding the clutter of spectators you swerve to miss a farmer's dog asleep in the road, a jangling herd of cows or some orange museum tractor built before the invention of speed. And you are aware you are in Aveyron - beautiful, bleak, soft, rugged, barren, fertile Aveyron. Paradox and contradiction. Proudly French and totally independent.

Aveyron is part of an ancient region once known as *le Rouergue*, which means quite literally 'red earth'. Its hills emanate like an afterthought from the high Auvergne before dwindling south into the equilibrium of Languedoc. There are four thousand kilometres of rivers and streams criss-crossing the land like veins. A quarter of Aveyron is forested, a rich natural resource and home to deer, wild boar and the binoculars of bird watchers. Overhead in the big skies, dominating the butterflies, wild meadows and vast lakes below, are the eagles, buzzards and red kites, wheeling and wheeler-dealing in the silence.

The fifth largest department in France, but its most secret. Cut off for centuries by its geography, by bands of outlaws and by outside neglect, it is a place which has had time to grow up in its own way. Time ticks with the slipping away of the seasons, not with a digital snap or the electric beeping of an alarm. The sound in your ears is that of an ancient tongue, strongly accented, weathered, articulating a piece of living history.

10 *Map of Aveyron*

AVEYRON

Main towns, rivers & geographical features

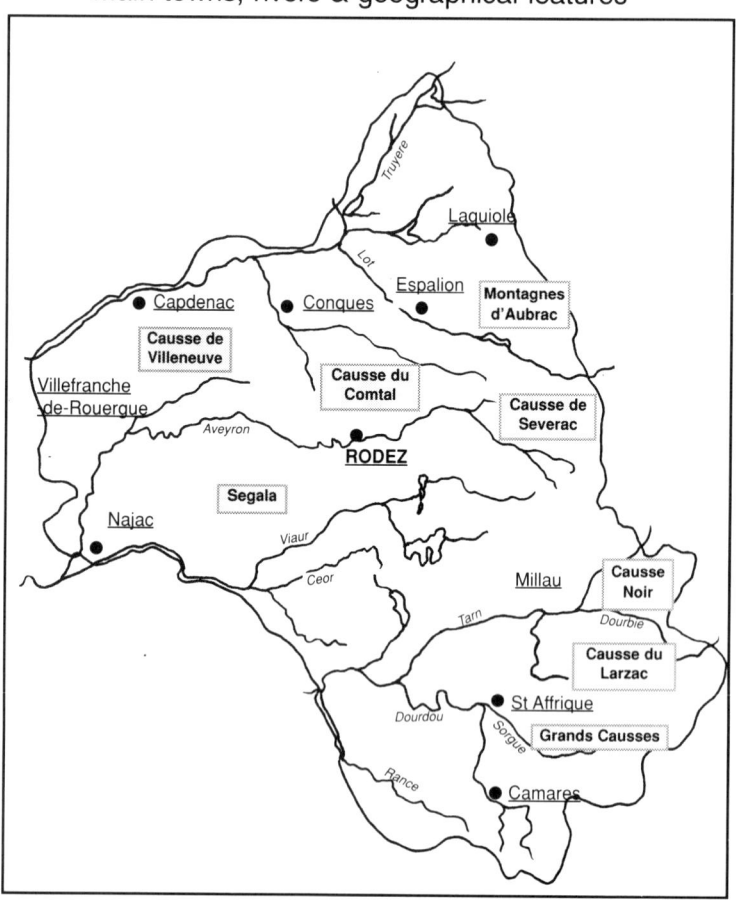

KEY

geographical feature | underlined town | *italics* river

INTRODUCTION

Living History

Why is there so often in Aveyron the feeling of being in a very ancient place?

Certainly it has something to do with knowing that human habitation here has been traced back to Neolithic times. It is also evident in the existence of the largest number of menhirs and dolmens in the whole of France. It is apparent through the fading imprints of ancient invaders - for the Rutènes, Romans, barbarians, Visigoths, Saracens, Cathars, English and Templars have all had a foothold in the region.

It is more subtly reinforced by the older slower pace of life in the villages and hamlets where the ancient langue d'Oc is still spoken. It is strongly sensed in the timeless transhumance of the Laguiole cattle to the Northern Montagne's summer pastures and in the southern plains and plateaux where sheep graze and provide milk for the Roquefort cheese.

But the real ancient and continuing history of Aveyron is to be found in the physical geography of the region itself. It is the unique formation of the land which gives the department its contrasts and its variety, both in the natural world and in the man-made.

Its relief has created three heights of land. The highest are in Montagne d'Aubrac in the north (up to 1450 metres); the outcrops or '*puechs*' of Lévezou in the centre (up to 1100 metres); and in the south certain parts of the Grand Causses of Larzac and Noir (up to 1000 metres). The second group are the more modest plateaux of the Ségala and the minor Causses of Comtal, Séverac and Rouge (between 500 - 800 metres). The lowest areas of land are the deep gorges and alluvial plains beside the rivers: Lot, Tarn, Truyère and Viaur (between 150 - 350 metres).

12 *Living History*

Similarly, an ancient twist of geology has given Aveyron three rock and soil types: *anciens, calcaires* and *volcaniques*. These affect not only the natural life and the agricultural specialisms of each area, but are also reflected in the local architecture's colours, materials and styles, from the deep red stones of Marcillac to the greys of Ségala and the almost black basalt in the Montagne.

In spite of the fact that man has created chequered fields, vast forests, huge lakes, roadways and centres of habitation, it is still the prehistoric formation of the natural landscape which dictates the ancient multiple personality of the character of Aveyron.

Hilltop château

At a Glance History of Aveyron

BC	700	Rutènes, a Gallic Tribe, settle in the area.
	52	Romans conquer Rouergue old Aveyron.
AD	4C	First Christian bishop of Rodez, Saint Amans.
	725	Saracens invade.
	12C	Numerous abbeys constructed.
	1252	Villefranche-de-Rouergeue founded by Alphonse de Poitiers.
	1281	Bastide of Sauveterre-de-Rouergue built.
	14/15C	Hundred Years War between England and France
	1561	Religious struggles between Catholics and Protestants begin around Villefranche-de-Rouergue and Millau.
	1615	Second religious war
	1628	Plague strikes Villefranche-de-Rouergue and Sauveterre.
	1789	French Revolution begins.

History at a Glance

1790	Formation of the department of Aveyron.
1808	The canton of St. Antonin becomes part of the newly formed department of Tarn-et-Garonne.
1834	The creation of Decazeville.
1854	Cholera epidemic.
1858	First railway opened from Montauban to Capdenac.
1860	Vines destroyed by phylloxera.
1886	Maximum recorded population of over 415,000 inhabitants.
1902	The viaduct over the Viaur opened.
1914/18	15,000 soldiers from Aveyron lost their lives in the Great War.
1942	Germans reach Rodez (liberated 1944).
1949	EDF constructs barrages on Le Lévezou.
1971	Uni-Air-Rouergue creates air link between Paris and Rodez.
1993	A75 reaches Aveyron.
1998	9 villages in Aveyron reach "*Plus Beaux Villages*" status, more than any other Department of France.

Administrative Divisions

Aveyron is the most easterly of the 8 departments in the area of South West France known as the Midi-Pyrenées, which extends to the Spanish border.

The department number for Aveyron is 12 - it is alphabetically the twelfth department of the 95 which make up the French Republic. (All five figure postcodes begin with and car number plates end with 12.)

Three *arrondisements*: Millau, Rodez and Villefranche -de-Rouergue.

These are the three largest centres of population. Rodez is the *Préfécture,* the capital. Each *arrondisement* is divided into *cantons.* Millau has 15 *cantons;* Rodez has 23; and Villefranche-de-Rouergue has 8.

Each *canton* is further subdivided into *communes.* In Millau this has resulted in 101 *communes;* In Rodez 139, and in Villfranche-de-Rouergue 64. This total of 304 *communes* divides further into hundreds of villages, hamlets and farms which, in all, house over 270,000 inhabitants.

The cantons are:

1. MILLAU
Belmont-sur Rance
Camares
Campagnac
Cornus
Millau (East and West)
Nant
Peyreleau
Saint-Affrique
Saint-Beauzely
Saint-Rome-de-Tarn
Saint-Sernin-sur-Rance
Salles-Curan
Severac-le-Chateau
Vezins-de-Levezou

2. RODEZ
Baraqueville
Bozouls
Cassagnes-Begonhes
Conques
Entraygues-sur-Truyere
Espalion
Estaing
Laguiole
Laissac
Marcillac-Vallon
Mur-de-Barrez
Naucelle
Pont-de-Salars
Requista
Rignac
Rodez (East, West and North)
Saint-Amans-des-Cots
Saint-Chely-d'Aubrac
Saint-Geniez-d'Olt
Sainte-Genevieve-sur-Argence
Salvetat-Peyrales

3. VILLEFRANCHE de ROUERGUE
Aubin
Capdenac-Gare
Decazeville
Montbazens
Najac
Rieupeyroux
Villefranche de Rouergue
Villeneuve

Villages

Following the French Revolution, the newly formed department of Aveyron (which replaced the former Rouergue) was initially divided up into 684 communes. This somewhat excessive number proved to be an administrative nightmare, not helped by the fact that the locals, conservative by nature, ignored the change and continued to refer to themselves as members of the old parishes! By the mid-nineteenth century the number of communes was reduced to 304, and only minor alterations to this system have been made since.

Each commune has a main town or village with its *mairie* and a small number of adjoining villages or hamlets, and will include farms in the vicinity. These function as a talking shop for local affairs and are a focus of local decision making

The enormous number of villages and hamlets in Aveyron reflects the power of the church and the land-owning nobility in previous centuries. Between 1050 and 1150 hundreds of churches were constructed around which villages and hamlets grew up, some of them fortified against wandering bands of robbers. Others developed around the lands of the great Franciscan and Dominican monasteries built in the thirteenth century. Still more were created by the great land owners.

The ancient houses in the villages and countryside of Aveyron reveal the story of the rural way of life of the past.

Very few of these original villages remain intact, though odd houses and churches have survived. Most suffered from attacks by invaders, destruction during the Hundred Years War with England and further damage during the Religious wars between Catholics and Protestants. So what exists now is as a result of frequent rebuilding and renovation over a period of some eight hundred years.

The main reason for the ancient 'feel', the charm and the unity of the Aveyron village, is the fact that over the past one hundred years very little has been added. Since the 1880s, when the population reached its maximum at little over 415,000, well over a third of the inhabitants have left the area - most for Paris in the late nineteenth century.

Dolmen

Red stone house

Cazelle

Timber framed house

Bastide town Sauveterre

Aubrac

Chestnut

Marcillac vine

Marcillac vineyard

Village gardens

Flower seller

Houses

First, the people wanted shelter from the cold winters and hot summers. So their homes were built with their backs to the north and with very small windows facing the southerly sun. In the oldest houses, the single roomed living accommodation was usually on the first floor, reached by external stone steps. It contained, at one end, the table and fireplace, overhung with hooks for meat and shelves suspended from ropes from the massive roof beams to keep food away from rodents. Around the rest of the room were cupboards, often cut out of the stone walls like little square caves, and beds for the family.

Many village houses are simple square fronted buildings, often in uneven terraces, constructed from large granite stones. Some were covered in rough rendering at one time, but now, more frequently, this rendering is being chipped away and the original walls are being tastefully pointed.

Others are constructed with timber framed and slightly overhanging top storeys. Again, in some places, the present owners are taking care to renovate these ancient facades. Although most houses adjoin one another, very rarely are they all alike. Only in the bastides is there any sense of uniformity of size and style.

Storage space was the second priority. In many houses, this was the function of the ground floor. In others, the chestnut crop or the wines and cheeses were kept in separate stone buildings. This ground floor space, later and in slightly more affluent times, became a place where animals were kept - supplying in winter a sort of under floor heating.

Thirdly, the combination of poverty and poor communication routes in the hilly areas meant that houses were built of stone hewn and shaped in the immediate locality. This factor accounts for the wide variety of colours to be found throughout Aveyron. Houses on the *causses* are almost white and golden, many are grey granite in the Viadène area between the Lot and Truyère rivers, and the villages in the wine-growing region of Marcillac-Vallon are a beautiful rich red.

The roofs too are of local material, each with its own style and colour. The wonderful roofscape of Conques is grey on a dull day, but shines with colours like oil on water in the sunshine.

In many villages the houses seem to be topped with overlapping lines of huge, thick grey biscuits, baked to a crumbly dryness at the edges. These are known as *lauzes* or *lauses*. Quite common in certain areas of Aveyron are the rounded topped lines of red tiles called *tuiles canal*.

Even the recent replacement roofs of man-made materials are more often than not carefully selected (and approved by the *mairie*) to fit in with the predominant style of the village. Of course, it must be remembered that the ancient buildings would once have been thatched - a type of roofing which no longer exists in Aveyron.

Farm Buildings

Farm buildings in this region vary enormously. High in the Aubrac there are what are known as *burons* - low stone built houses which are used by the farmers who bring their cattle to the high summer pastures in May. They're also used as tiny temporary cheese factories and a few serve passing travellers with home-made *aligot* at tables under trees. Completely uninhabited, but still standing in many parts of western Aveyron and on some *causses* are tiny, circular, dry-stone walled shelters for shepherds known as *cazelles*

Some of the richer farmers of the past constructed all their buildings (the farmhouse, stables, barns) around a central courtyard, which was entered through a roofed archway, often with tower and pigeon loft to one side. Although the vast majority are still at the heart of working farms, a few have been renovated by new owners to provide unique living accommodation. You'll see many examples of this type of farm complex around the Villefranche-de-Rouergue area.

Some smaller farms have just two adjoining buildings - the house and the barn. Often, the current generation of farmers have opted to build themselves new homes and allow the old family home adjacent to fall into ruin.

Over the past twenty years with the advent of tourism in Aveyron, numerous country and village properties, perhaps left empty for years, have been completely renovated and updated to provide holiday homes and *gîte* accommodation of a high standard, some with their own swimming pools.

Châteaux

Every other village in Aveyron has what's called a *château,* though in most cases this hardly translates as 'castle'. They would perhaps be better described as small manor houses. This is not to say, however, that there are no real castles in the department.

> You'll find a couple of splendid examples of Renaissance castles near Villefranche-de-Rouergue and on the tops of rocky hills you'll see some wonderful fortresses, quite apart from the remains of parts of *chateaux* and their fortifications incorporated into more recent buildings.

Bastides

It was Alphonse de Poitiers, brother of St Louis (King Louis IX of France), who was credited with originating the idea of the bastide town in the middle of the thirteenth century. In 1252, he gave orders to begin work on two bastides, at Villeneuve-sur-Lot and at Villefranche-de-Rouergue, the first of their type to be constructed.

These new towns represented a departure from the usual urban way of life. To the individual there were many obvious advantages in living in one of these fortified towns. The rights enjoyed weren't democratic in the sense the word is understood today, but they gave those fortunate enough to enjoy them an escape from the numbing shackles of feudalism.

People living within a bastide were roughly equal, having property and land of similar proportions, each being allowed an 8 metre front - the span of an arcade arch around the central square. Franchises and privileges were granted by means of an officially recorded charter. The rights granted by such charters included the right to elect councillors, the right to dispose of property, the right to mill flour and to bake bread without having to pay taxes and the right to the protection of their lord without having to serve in his or any other army. In feudal times, these rights were considerable.

But the creation of these new bastides gave Alphonse de

Poitiers an advantage too, that of power in areas where otherwise he was powerless. When, through marriage, he inherited a large area of Aquitaine, he discovered that the lands he had title to were in fact ruled by other lords who offered him little other than allegiance to his title. To combat this, he established military strongholds known as *chatelleries* and the the fortified bastide towns throughout his domaine which were to become of enormous economic, political and military significance. The idea was copied by others, most notably by the kings of England and France. During the thirteenth and fourteenth centuries, they created hundreds of these fortified towns in order to consolidate their respective positions of power.

Bastides were constructed to a common plan, though in some instances existing buildings or unique geography meant that changes had to be made. The early bastides were built in river valleys but later, when fortification became paramount, they were built mainly on the tops of hills. Generally, the towns were constructed around a central square, which served as market and meeting place, the streets leading from it were planned on a grid system which extended to the town's walls and fortified gateways. Along each street were houses built on equal sized plots of land, and those around the central square had stone arcades on the bottom floor wide enough to allow for the passage of a cart.

In Rouergue (the old name for the area which now comprises Aveyron), there are four major examples of bastides, each one is slightly different according to its history and geography. They are Villefranche-de-Rouergue, built in a river valley on the original orders of Alphonse de Poitiers and the largest; Najac, perched on its unique hilltop site; Villeneuve-d'Aveyron, grafted onto an older monastery and church; and Sauveterre-de-Rouergue, which is perhaps a copybook example of its type.

Najac castle

The Food

Les Fromages

There are four well known cheeses produced in the Aveyron - Roquefort, Bleu des Causses, Laguiole and the Cantal de Thérondels - but, as in the rest of France, you can buy famous varieties of cheese from other regions in the shops, markets and supermarkets. Most cheese sold is of a good standard as you might expect in a country where people eat more cheese per head of population than any other in the world.

Roquefort renowned as one of the world's supreme blue cheeses is matured in the naturally occuring caves in the commune of Roquefort-sur-Soulzon at very low temperatures. The cheese is made from full cream, unpasteurised ewes' milk which is collected throughout the area and other parts of France with a similar climate and agriculture. The cheese itself, however, is always manufactured and matured at Roquefort-sur-Souzon in conditions which gives the finished cheese its unique flavour. The natural caves, which to the visitor can resemble an underground city, have within them a fine mist which ensures a perpetually damp atmosphere and a permanent low temperature (6 - 8 degrees centigrade) which allows the *penicillin roqueforti* to develop, creating a wonderful marbling effect in the cheese.

When buying Roquefort always look for a creamy yellow flesh with a good even marbling, called *persillage* - avoid crumbly cheeses which have a too white or grey white flesh. If in doubt, always ask for a taste. '*Est-ce-que je peux goûter?*' It is only what the vendor would expect from his customers anyway.

Bleu des Causses, as its name suggests, is the other blue cheese from the region, but unlike Roquefort it is manufactured from unpasteurised cows' milk. Matured in the caves of Peyrelade for a period of between 3 - 6 months, it is made like a round loaf about 20 centimetres in diameter and 8 - 10 centimeters deep with a flowery crust. Neither pressed nor cooked, the finished cheese is moister and more crumbly than other French blue cheeses and is less salty than Roquefort. The rules of *appellation d'origine controllé* (AOC, which is stamped on the foil) insist that every cheese remains in the limestone caves for a minimum of 70 days and only those which reach the right standard will be approved for sale. Local chefs often use Bleu des Causses for adding to omelettes and crêpes.

Laguiole

Laguiole is produced high up on the plateau of the Aubrac and is made from unpasteurised, full cream cows' milk. The cheese is usually allowed to mature for four months at a temperature which does not exceed 14 degrees centigrade, though it can be eaten at various stages of maturity. To the British or American palate it is a firm, mild cheese, golden in colour, not dissimilar to cheddar and can be cooked with in the same way. Though perhaps it is most delicious just eaten simply as it is with fresh bread and a glass of local red wine.

Cantal de Thérondels

Cantal de Thérondels is not unlike Laguiole and is virtually identical to the Cantal produced in the neighbouring Auvergne. The local cooperative has 22 members who traditionally manufacture the cheese using unpasteurised milk from Saler and Aubrac cattle. Like cheddar it has three strengths of taste, but instead of mild, medium and mature can be bought *jeune* (between 30 - 90 days old), *entre deux* (between 90 - 180 days old) and *vieux* (180 days plus). *Tome fraîche* for Aligot is also produced. Cantal is a firm cheese which is very popular throughout France. This local version is in no way inferior to that of its neighbour and is worth looking out for in the shops and markets.

As well as these

As well as these, other less well known cheeses are produced in the region and sold either by small producers at the point of production or from stalls in the open air markets. Cheeses manufactured *à la fermière* (on the farm) in this way usually signifies that the process involves the use of *lait cru*, unpasteurised milk. Whereas if a cheese is produced *à la laiterie*, it is probably made in a factory from pasteurised milk. If you can buy a cheese *à la fermière* so much the better, because there really is no comparison in terms of taste. But again try the cheeses out for yourself in the markets or at the farms where you see cheeses advertised for sale.

Many of the little farms produce

only goats' cheese. This makes sense for two reasons - economically, because goats produce twice as much milk as cows and, productively, because an average goats' cheese is much more straightforward to make, possessing none of the the intricacies and mysteries involved in creating a Roquefort. The resulting product is usually good and satisfying without reaching the dizzy heights of an outstanding cheese. The small hard round cheeses are certainly worth buying, tending to be more tasty than their soft counterparts. Cool goats' cheese makes an excellent lunch on a hot day and lightly toasted and accompanied by a simple salad can make an excellent entrée or snack. A goats' cheese well worth sampling is the **Cabécou du Fel** from the Pays d'Olt.

In Villefranche-de-Rouergue, a very rich, very delicious, full fat, soft cheese is produced, called **St André**. It is not to be recommended, however, if you're on a diet but it is definitely worth trying as a delicious, cholesterol packed end to your meal. Because of its moist texture, it is probably not worth trying to take back with you at the end of the holiday and is to be only really enjoyed in Aveyron

From high in the Aubrac and in the neighbouring region of Cantal in the Auvergne comes **Tome Fraîche**. This is usually produced and thus only obtainable during the spring and summer months when it can either be eaten fresh or cooked as part of a delicious local dish called **Aligot**. Tome is a cheese which has not been fermented and is slightly sour

Aligot

To make this dish you need about 1 kilo of old potatoes, slighlty under 1/2 kilo of Tome Fraîche de Laguiole (roughly 2 - 3 days old), 2 - 3 tablespoons of crème fraîche, 1/4 kilo of butter, 3 - 4 (or more!) cloves of garlic, salt to taste.

Cook the potatoes in salt water until they are soft, then mash to a fine puree. While the potatoes are cooking, cut the Tome Fraîche into fine slices and finely chop or, if you prefer, crush the garlic in a mortar and pestle. Mix the

> butter and the crème fraîche with the pureed potatoes and reheat, adding any necessary salt. As the mixture warms over a low heat, stir in the Tome Fraîche and the garlic vigorously until it has completely melted and blended in. The locals say that if you want to make your Aligot taste a bit special you must at this stage stir in a little duck or goose fat for added flavour.

when eaten fresh but perfect in taste and texture when its is prepared as follows:

In the *burons* of the Aubrac, it is still possible to taste Aligot at the place where the cheese is produced. *Burons* are low stone buildings, originally thatched, now roofed with *lauzes* (oval roof slates), used by farmers in summer as temporary housing and small cheese factories. They are well worth visiting if you have an interest in cheese production on a small scale and certainly worth visiting for a substantial lunch.

Le Stockfish

In modern day Aveyron fresh and frozen fish, with gills or in shells, is widely available in the fish shops and supermarkets of the towns, but this was not the case in its poverty stricken, land-locked past. Apart from fresh water fish, such as trout, pike and carp, the only salt water fish available to the Aveyronaise was something known as *Le Stockfish*. Stockfish is cod, haddock or hake which has been gutted and hung up to dry for sometimes as much as a year until it is as hard and stiff as a piece of wood. It is believed that it was introduced into the area by Rouergat soldiers returning from war with the Dutch during the reign of Louis XIV, which would explain why it is thought that the word 'stock' derived from Old Dutch meaning 'piece of wood'.

To rehydrate a *stockfish* it is necessary to soak it for a week regularly changing the water. Modern housewives prefer to cook with *la morue,* salt cod, which requires only twenty four hours soaking before it can be used. Surprisingly enough dried and salted cod are still used in the region and can be seen hanging not just from stalls in the traditional open air markets and in fishmongers but in the supermarkets in the towns as well.

Le stockfish or its substitute, salt cod, forms the main ingredient of a delicious local dish called *l'Estofinado,* which is a speciality of Villefranche-de-Rouergue and Decazeville. Because it is so difficult to prepare, for after cooking and soaking the fish flesh has to be carefully flaked and pounded to a pulp, the dish is usually only prepared for special occasions or by restaurants.

L'Estofinado offers the opportunity of sampling one of the authentic dishes of the past and is delicious.

L'Estofinado

The ingredients are dried or salted fish, potatoes, eggs, walnut oil, milk, garlic, parsley and seasoning.

The pulped fish is added to the mashed potatoes over a very low heat, followed in order by milk, parsley, beaten raw eggs and heated walnut oil. The mixture is beaten until it has the texture of a light puree when, after seasoning, it is ready for immediate serving, perhaps garnished with slices of hard-boiled egg.

Fouace

Although Fouace, like the ubiquitous *tarte au prune*, is found throughout South West France from the Dordogne to the Pyrenees, for Aveyron it does possess a cultural as well as a culinary significance. Described by some as little more than bread made with eggs and sugar, for like bread it is baked in a bread oven with yeast used as a raising agent, this lowly cake formed an important part in the past in celebrating saints' days and festivals in the Christian calendar.

Today, it is eaten at celebratory events, such as weddings and christenings, or partaken of in the late afternoon with a glass of sweet white wine to counteract the cake's dryness.

In Najac each year, on the Sunday following the 15th August, a giant *fouace* is towed through the town by truck, accompanied by music and dancers as part of the town's weekend festival. Both the festival and the town are well worth visiting, but I wouldn't lose any sleep if you never get to taste a *fouace*.

Tripou

Tripou is sold throughout the region, but is a particular favourite of the eastern Rodez area towards Séverac-le-Château, where it goes especially well with the Marcillac wine, and around Naucelle, south of Rodez, where you'll find the award-winning **Tripou Charles-Savy**.

It is made from tripe and ham simmered in a sauce of white wine, carrots, tomatoes, celery, herbs and spices. The tripes, usually sheep's, but sometimes veal, are cut into rectangles, stuffed with the diced meat and some of the tripe and then tied into little parcels to cook slowly in the sauce for up to eight hours. In the past, the dish was placed in a cooling bread oven to cook over night.

A special kind of *tripou, les trénels,* is served in restaurants all around the Millau area. It is prepared with tripe, ham, herbs, tomatoes and white wine. It can be bought fresh from the butchers/charcutiers and is occasionally found tinned by local producers. Tinned *tripou* only requires warming up and, if you like that sort of thing, tastes very good.

Les Truffes

Usually it is the Perigord which is associated with truffles, but Aveyron too has its secret stores of these highly prized 'black diamonds'. Truffles are a fungus which grow underground during the winter by attaching themselves to the root of a tree, usually an oak below thirty to thirty five years old. They are snouted out by pigs which are fed tiny morsels of truffle to encourage their sense of smell, but dogs can also be trained to root for them.

You can find truffles on sale in Villefranche-de-Rouergue market on a Thursday morning in March and in the town's restaurants and the causse de Villeneuve area. They are also found on the causses near Millau, Nant, Peyreleau and Cornus where they may feature in the local cuisine at that time of year - most probably in an omelette.

The fact that truffles are not cultivated and are also extremely difficult to find contributes in no small degree to making them the world's most expensive food - fetching, even in the local area, over £100.00 a pound. And if you're thinking of bringing some home, don't be fooled into thinking that the tinned version will taste as special as the original - it won't!

Les Champignons

About 80 different kinds of edible fungi grow in France, many of which you will find growing in Aveyron if you are brave enough to look. Brave enough, that is, in two senses - one, that your indentification and selection will not end you up in hospital and, two, that you dare to 'trespass' on one of the most precious of Frenchman's preserves, the fungi patch. Searching for edible fungi is a very serious activity and you would have to get up very early in the morning to beat a local aficionado to gather these field and woodland prizes.

At the appropriate time of year, you can often obtain many of the varieties from the local markets stalls or even from greengrocers. It is unlikely that you will find the harmless though deadly sounding *trompettes de la mort* on sale, though you will find *cépes* (boletus), *mousserons, pleurotes* (oyster mushrooms), and, of course, trumpet shaped *chanterelles*. You may also be lucky enough to find the *morille* (morel) with its brown, pitted head, thought by many to be the only fungi to come close to the truffle in flavour. If you are lucky enough to find some, remember that morels need cooking to neutralise the poison they contain and should not be eaten raw.

Picking and preparing delicacies such as these should really remain the preserve of those in the know - but anyone can learn. Even the French take the precaution of having the chemists shop operate a fungi indentification service on behalf of the local community, to the extent of sometimes opening on Sundays. During the main picking season, it is not unusual either for chemist shop windows to be full of models of all the edible varieties for keen gatherers to check their harvest against. This is how serious the French are about *Les Champignons* - the name, incidentally, they give to all fungi not just to mushrooms.

Les Noix

Chestnut trees once grew in this area prolifically and their fruit served as food for both the people and their animals. Two hundred years ago the inhabitants of a very poor region of Aveyron, called Ségala, were known as *les ventres noirs* (the black bellies) because of their reliance on bread made from mainly rye and chestnuts as the basis for their nearly starvation diet.

Now, for a variety of reasons, such as a disease called *l'encre* (ink) and over exploitation of the wood for commercial purposes, the importance of the chestnut as part of the everyday diet has declined. It remains possible to buy chestnuts at harvest time in the open air markets and at local greengrocers, evidence that they continue to be used in home cuisine and in some restaurants.

Fouace, tarts and cakes made with chestnuts are still on sale in the patisseries of the department but such baking is not widespread and you will have to keep your eyes open to discover it. Worth looking for also is a liqueur which is made by combining chestnuts, strong *eau de vie*, a little water, vanilla and sugar should you desire to sip a little something from Aveyron's disappearing past.

There are two sorts of chestnut - the cultivated *marron,* which has a single husk containing its single nut, and the wild *châtaigne* which is smaller and flatter and whose nuts are contained in two or three husks. Most chestnuts today are bought in cans, but these are likely to be from the Ardeche which is the main production centre for chestnuts in France.

Walnut

trees also flourish in Aveyron. Although the Dordogne valley with its milder, less extreme climate is more favourable to their cultivation. The walnut is a more affluent version of the chestnut and can be consumed raw, pressed into oil or as a part of other dishes such as salad.

Oil from pressed walnuts tends to have a strong flavour and is used in *l'Estofinado* to give it edge. A factory produced version of walnut oil is produced though this is inferior to and keeps less well than the real farm pressed version, both are readily available but it is worth paying a little extra for quality.

Throughout the region many restaurants offer as a starter a salad which is sometimes called a *salade rouergate* and others a *salade aveyronaise*. This local salad contains walnuts, walnut oil and is refreshing, delicious and stimulating to the taste buds. As the beginning to a meal consisting of local cuisine, it is perfect. In its various forms this salad can contain lettuce, tomatoes, wine vinegar, walnut oil, Roquefort cheese and walnuts. Its overall effect is wonderful and well worth repeating.

Les Canards et Les Oies

From the feathers to the *foie gras* to the fat, every morsel of the Aveyronian duck and goose is either put to good use or consumed. The birds are a significant part of the rural life of the area - in its farming, its markets, its forests and festivals, its commerce, its local specialities and its methods of cooking.

On almost every menu in the region, you'll see *confits de canard* or *confits d'oie* as a main course, usually served with potatoes fried in duck or goose fat, often with a sauce or a vegetable chosen to counteract the richness of the meat, such as a tomato and caper sauce or the rather bitter puree of sorrel leaves. The *confits* are made by first salting the portions of the bird for twenty four hours, then very slowly simmering them in their previously rendered fat for at least a couple of hours in a large pan. They're then cooled, covered with strained fat and kept in tightly sealed preserving jars. Later, they can be re-heated or eaten cold with a salad dressed with walnut oil.

The *magret* (breast) *de canard* is popular throughout France, cooked quickly and served slightly pink. Its local success in Aveyron is due to the quality of the meat and the thick layer of fat which occurs only in the ducks which have been specially fattened to increase the size of their livers for *foie gras*. (This process is known as *gavage* and many farms invite visitors to come and watch the birds being force-fed, either by the ancient method of maize-filled funnels or by modern mechanisation.)

Before going on to look at the complexities of buying *foie gras*, it's worth mentioning what traditionally happens to the rest of the bird. The *abattis* (giblets: neck, gizzard and heart) can be simmered with vegetables and herbs in a simple stew served with hearty regional bread. The neck itself is often served boned and stuffed with minced pork, duck, liver or *foie gras*. As a starter, you'll see warm gizzard salad on the menus, called *salade de gesiers*. Bits of meat picked off the carcass are called *fritons* and are often served at village celebratory dinners with an aperitif. Tiny slices of skin from the *confits* are browned and used in omelettes. Other morsels of meat and fat are made into *rillettes de canard* served as a main course with potatoes or on toast with an aperitif. Even the carcass itself is used for stock or grilled in pieces for a little tasty nibble. Of course the feathers are used to stuff pillows and cushions.

You'll see the entire birds for sale alive or dead (with or without livers) in many markets, especially from November to the New Year. You'll also find stalls selling trays of cooked pieces, bottled and tinned specialities and fresh *magrets* vacuum sealed in polythene. There could also be fresh and dried duck saussage and smoked duck breasts.

You may be surprised and pleased to discover most of these delicacies also for sale in local supermarkets and out-of-town hypermakets, which are far more regional in their product lines than their British counterparts.

Finally, the livers. These are absolutely delicious cooked fresh and eaten warm, but more often than not, you'll come across them in restaurants served cold.

Markets, supermarkets, butchers and charcuteries sell various liver-based products in tins, bottled or sliced from large moulds. The purest, best and most expensive is the f*oie gras de canard entier* (or goose) either well or lightly cooked. (*cuit* or *mi-cuit*.) Next, there's a *bloc de foie gras* which is reconstituted and shaped. It should be eaten very cold. Then there are *terrines de canard au foie gras* and duck meat and liver *terrines* flavoured with orange, armagnac or shallots. Many terrines and pates are a mixture of duck and pork, as are the *galantines de foie de canar*d which are actually a fifty-fifty mixture of duck liver and chopped pork.

If you're unsure, ask the vendor or read the label carefully - it'll give you the ingredients and the percentages of each meat. To get a real flavour of the products, it's a good idea to visit one of the local producers who will take time to explain the ingredients and the cooking methods as well as giving you a free taste. The best, like **á la ferme Carles** at Monteils, cook to traditional recipes (with no colourings or preservatives) often over a wood fire.

Les Vins

Marcillac

The red wine of Marcillac is unique among French wine in so far as it is the only wine to be made one hundred per cent from a grape variety known widely as *fer servadou*, or *mansois* as it called in the local occitaine dialect. The wines from this region have been improving greatly over the past few decades and this has been rewarded recently by the granting of *appellation d'origine controllé* status. If it was not for the European Union's policy which is designed to restrict wine over-production, Marcillac would have been able to expand significantly and, what is more, been able to sell the increase in output with little problem.

In the mid-sixties Marcillac wine was almost forgotten, but through the energy and initiative of the cave cooperative, run by André Metge, wine production in the area is once again flourishing and lucrative. The *cave cooperative* functions by taking the grapes which local producers have to offer and processing them into wine. Many of the grape producers who form part of the *cave cooperative* do not grow vines as their sole cash crop but rely on grape production for only part of their income.

Indeed, there are only three independent producers who concentrate solely on wine production - Pierre Locombe, Philippe Teulier and Jean-Luc Matha. The last two of these are great friends and great rivals who have pushed Marcillac wines to new heights of development. Philippe Teulier has introduced modern techniques into his wine making, but even so while half his *remontage* - the process involving the grape skins being submerged in liquid - is done by machine, the other half is still done by using his feet . His red wines are of a very good standard and well worth looking out for. Jean-Luc Matha's wines, on the other hand, are generally fuller as they have undergone a longer *cuvaison* of fifteen days. The reds produced in the region are very blackcurranty and can age well. Jean-Luc Matha keeps his reds in barrels for up to a year and newly bottled are excellent drunk slightly chilled with and an appropriate *entrée*. Only the reds have AOC status, but the *rosés* and Monsieur Matha's white vin de table are interesting and warrants a gulp or two - you'll drink much worse.

The Vallée de Vallon is an extremely beautiful part of Aveyron and offers the visitor much with its steep terraces, views and red stone villages. So, if you're in the area and as nothing really substitutes for tasting the wine yourself, why not stop off at the little vineyards to see if its worth taking a few bottles away. You will be most welcome.

Entraygues et le Fel

At the place where the River Truyère meets the River Lot after its descent from the high Montagnes, stands the beautiful town of Entraygues-sur-Truyère with its castle and thirteenth century river bridge. It is in the high hills surrounding the town and a tiny village, nearby Le Fels, where the vines are cultivated, breathing the clear mountain air and the warm winds of the Mediterranean.

The total area of vines is small, amounting to little more than twenty hectares and, given the precipitous nature of the terrain, largely picked by hand as to get machinery onto the terraces would be impossible. The small quantity of wine produced is extremely popular in the area and is consumed locally by the Aveyronais and the Auvergnats of Cantal. The Auvergnats, renowned as the bistro and cafe owners of Paris, sold wines in their establishments in the capital with which they were familiar, Entraygues et Le Fels was always one of the more popular.

Wine producers are still countable on one hand and, even though there has been an effort to elevate the region's VDQS status to the more lofty AOC, there would seem to be little point given the healthy sales the wine enjoys and the difficulty involved in harvesting. The terrain would make increased productivity very difficult.

Like most regions there are three types of wine produced - red, white and rosé. The red wine, unlike that of Marcillac, is not produced from a single grape or, indeed, from a standard grape *assemblage* but can, for instance, be a mixture of *mansois, cabernet franc* and *gamay* at one vineyard and *gamay, jurançon noir, cabernet franc* and *negret* at another. The lesson is always to taste to try to find the one which appeals to you most, especially if you are buying more than the single bottle.

The white wines, on the other hand, are made solely from a grape variety called *chenin blanc* and are of a very good quality. They tend to be very dry to the taste and have a combination of lemony, appley, almondy flavours. They go well with smoked or fresh fish and with seafood. Although it is generally thought the white needs to be drunk young, it will in fact age well.

The *rosés* are pleasant and go well, served chilled, with local cuisine. But if you get the chance to try just one of the wines of the area, go for the white - you won't be disappointed. **Six or a dozen bottles would not represent an extravagant investment to take home!**

Estaing

Estaing is a tiny wine producing area in the Pays D'Oll and claims to be the smallest producer of VDQS wines in the whole of France, with only 15 hectares under cultivation and with only three independent producers and a *cave cooperative*. The independent producers share a common label, with their printed names the only clue to the difference in the origin of the contents.

Red, white and rosé wines are produced, but only the cave cooperative and Monique Fages produce a white, which is a mixture of *chenin blanc* and *mauzac* and a bit of an acquired taste. The reds go well with local regional cooking, especially with *Aligot*.

Estaing produces good, honest country wines made in a traditional way. Sometimes the lack of modern equipment means that a sediment is evident floating in some of the wines but this is quite harmless and, in a world increasingly oppressed by the insipidity of mass production, only contributes to its honesty.

Vintage is not recorded on the bottles as every year the total production is sold. What better endorsement!

Try it, it is different.

Vins des Gorges et Côtes de Millau

Once an area of production covering 1500 hectares and producing 500,000 hectolitres of wine, it was greater in size than the vineyards of modern day Bergerac and had a reputation which stretched as far as New York. Following phylloxera, two World Wars and the frost of 1956, the area of production today is a modest 100 hectares but the fact it survived at all is a tribute to the resilience of the local growers and the soil's ability to grow grapes better than any other crop.

Following an unsuccessful flirtation with lower quality wine earlier in the century, the wines from this region obtained VDQS status in 1994 which represented a lot of work undertaken to raise the quality of the local production. Now local wine must hold its own in an increasingly competetitive arena and a reliable product is the only way of ensuring a future for itself.

The name hardly trips off the tongue, but it can't call its output Vin de Gorge du Tarn because Tarn is the name of another department which has its own vins de pays Des Côtes du Tarn. Its terraces located, nevertheless, in the Gorge du Tarn are planted with a variety of grapes for making reds and *rosés - cabernet franc, gamay, syrah* and a small variety of local grapes, such as *malbec* and *negret* - and *chenin blanc* and *mauzan* for making the white wine, one not unlike an Entraygues. Again the wines from this region, like those of the others, go well with robust local food.

Marcillac Vineyard

USEFUL INFORMATION

Tourism

There are three factors which account for the slowly increasing popularity of Aveyron as a holiday centre for both French and foreign visitors.

First, compared with coastal resorts and other more established tourist areas, it is not expensive to live here. With its declining population and lack of large industries, Aveyron has been one of the poorest departments of France this century. In rural areas, life is still very simple. The towns do not display the affluence of those in the more prosperous north of the country but they do offer a wide variety of interesting small shops, run by local traders rather than chain-stores. Most places will have an inexpensive local market and supermarkets. Only outside the largest towns will you find a range of cut price furniture stores, garden centres, DIY chains and hypermarkets.

Second, there is an excellent choice of places to stay all very competitively priced. There are about 200 hotels, a similar number of *chambres d'hôtes,* over 25 *villages de vacances* and countless places to camp, from farmers' fields to four star sites, both privately and municipally run. Fastest growing, however, is the *gîte* holiday. Many companies in the UK are now beginning to cover this area, and some British owned properties are advertised privately in newspapers or in specialist magazines. The largest choice, and perhaps best bargains, are to be found either through local listings from French organisations (such as **Gîtes de France** and **Cléconfort**) or by contacting local *Offices de Tourisme* or *Syndicats d'Initiative.*

The third, most significant factor is that Aveyron is an area in which to enjoy *le tourisme vert.* The rich patrimony and natural diversity of the countryside, the clean air, unpolluted fish filled rivers and streams, the wild flowers, birds and above all the quiet, lend to the region a simplicity and straightforwardness which has disappeared from so many other once admirable places. This is not a region for discos or a pulsing night life, here visitors enjoy simple pleasures, such as walking, fishing, canoeing, cycling, sailing, climbing, caving, horse riding, sightseeing and, of course, the eating and drinking. Now, the department has begun even to put its cold winters to some advantage. Increasingly, during the cold months, the Aubrac is becoming a popular ski destination, offering the jaded traveller an uncomplicated, good value break.

Tourist Information

Many towns and villages, even some very small ones, have tourist information offices. These are an invaluable source of up to the minute information for the independent traveller. Usually someone in attendance will speak some English, but don't take this service for granted. Anyway, you can usually help yourself to the material you need without assistance, as leaflets and colour brochures are clearly on display. Though these probably will be in French, so take your phrasebook if you need one.

Tourist information offices will help you find out the dates, times and locations of fairs, fetes, pageants, arts events, communal banquets and historical venues. They are a source of information on local transport as well as having details of canoe and kayak hire, rafting, the whereabouts of golf courses, tennis courts, riding stables and swimming pools, with directions, costs and opening times. Finally, they can offer lists of hotels, restaurants, camp sites and will have the addresses of local *gîtes* for hire at well below prices on offer in the UK.

You will notice that these tourist information offices have two different titles, either they a called an Office de Tourisme or a Syndicat d'Initiative, but there is no need to worry because they both do the same thing.

Arcades at Sauveterre

Aveyron is divided up for the purposes of tourism into 8 distinct areas:

1. **Aubrac, Carladez, Vallée du Lot**
Regional Office - Espalion 12500
tel. 05 65 44 10 63 / fax. 05 65 48 02 57

2. **Conques-Marcillac**
Regional Office - Conques 12320
tel. 05 65 72 85 00 / fax. 05 65 72 87 03

3. **Des gorges de l'Aveyron à la vallée du Lot**
Regional Office - Villefranche-de-Rouergue
12200 tel. 05 65 45 13 18 / fax.05 65 45 55 58

4. **Rodez et la vallée de l'Aveyron**
Regional Office - Rodez 12005
tel. 05 65 68 02 27 / fax. 05 65 68 78 15

5. **Monts et lacs du Lévezou**
Regional Office - Pont-de-Salars 12290
tel. 05 65 46 82 46

6. **Ségala- pays du Viaur**
Regional Office - Naucelle 12800
tel. 05 65 47 04 32

7. **Millau grands causses**
Regional Office - Millau 12100
tel. 05 65 60 02 42 / fax. 05 65 61 36 08

8. **Roquefort et Saint-Affricain**
Regional office - Saint-Affrique 12400
tel. 05 65 99 09 05 / fax. 05 65 58 91 44

For pre-departure tourist information you can contact The French Tourist Office

21/24 Grosvenor Place,
London. SW1 7HU

Tel. 0891 244123

You can also use this number to get in touch with the **Gîte de France** organisation

Getting There/ Getting Around

By Road
Having crossed the channel by ferry or through the channel tunnel, there are three main ways into Aveyron. The first is to the east by the Autoroute A75 from the Paris direction. Here you exit either at Massiac, taking the N122 to Aurillac and on to the Aubrac or further south at St. Flour, taking the D921 towards Rodez. Also you can remain on the A75, direction Rodez and, Millau, and continue towards the Causse du Larzac. The second follows the good N roads straight through the middle of France, via Le Mans, then joining the new A20 at Chateauroux, driving past Limoges and Brive and heading for Figeac or Cahors *en route* to Villefranche-de-Rouergue or through Figeac to Rodez. The third possibility is to pass through South West France to Toulouse from the northern Spanish ferry port at Santander. From Toulouse you can either take the N20 or A62 to Montauban and then on to Villefranche-de-Rouergue or the A68 to Gaillac and then on the N88 via Albi into Aveyron or the D922 from Gaillac towards Laguepie and Villefranche-de-Rouergue.

By Rail
You can take the Eurostar to Paris from where there is a through train daily to Aveyron and several others which involve changes. It is perhaps worth noting that there is an excellent night sleeper to Paris which leaves from Najac or Villefranche-de-Rouergue before midnight to arrive in the capital at about seven in the morning. If you want help and booking advice regarding Eurostar and travelling on the French railway, then call 0990 848848.

Use the same number for booking Motor Rail

By Air
There are regular flights from the UK to Toulouse, or from Paris to Rodez- Marcillac. It is advisable to check specific fly drive facilities at each of the airports when booking.

The addresses and phone numbers of the French airports are:

Aéroport international
Toulouse-Blagnac
31700 BLAGNAC
Tel. 05 61 62 44 00

Aéroport Rodez-Marcillac
route de Decazeville
12330 SALLES-LA-SOURCE
Tel. 05 65 76 02 00

Public transport

Travelling between the main towns in Aveyron is not a problem as there is a good bus service, supplemented in some places by the remains of a railway service. But to get to the hamlets, villages and smaller towns is much more problematic if you don't have your own means of transport. There is a skeletal bus service which runs to the more remote areas but don't expect it to operate daily, even during the summer months. If you want unfettered travel outside of the main centres and you want to see as much as possible then you'll need your own car, motorbike, bicycle, canoe or any combination to get the most out of your time here.

Tourist offices will supply you with up to the minute information regarding all local transport.

On Foot

With the aid of the appropriate *Serie Bleue* map, you can follow the lanes and designated footpaths throughout the department. Many Tourist Offices will stock pamphlets of local walks and others are produced by the *Comité departémental de la Randonnée Pédestre*, the local association of the national Ramblers' group. Their headquarters is in Rodez, 33 rue Victor-Hugo. (tel 05 65 68 88 60)

Maps

Once you are in Aveyron, it is well worth buying a copy of a map of the department. Perhaps the best is called **Aveyron Carte Touristique de L'Espace et du Patrimonie**. It can be obtained in advance from CDT, Maison du Tourisme, 6 place Jean-Jaurès, 12009 Rodez (Tel. 05 65 75 55 70). This map shows all the little D roads which form a kind of drunken spider's web between the main roads which interconnect the towns.

If you're intending to do any exploration of a particularly small area by car, bike or on foot, it's advisable to have the relevant **Série Bleue** map which shows in detail all the lanes, footpaths and buildings. Indeed, if you're thinking of exploring the lanes of western Aveyron in 'the land of a thousand streams', don't contemplate setting off without the relevant map for the area or you could have a very frustrating day.

The line maps in this book are designed to give you an idea of the places worth visiting from the main towns, directions and the main roads to follow. But don't be fooled into thinking any road in Aveyron is straight.

Climate

Because of the large difference in altitude between northern and southern Aveyron, the climate varies considerably too. The altitude in Aubrac is over 1,000 metres, whereas in Saint-Affrique it is only 330 metres. Consequently, Aubrac has twice as much rainfall and is, throughout the year, at least four degrees centigrade colder.

During the main holiday period in July and August, you can expect some very hot days with temperatures in excess of thirty degrees. You may also be there to experience some incredible thunder storms and torrential rain though these do not generally last very long and often occur at night.

The weather in winter time is very unpredictable, though you can guarantee snow on the higher ground to the north and east where skiing is becoming increasingly popular. Lower down, it can often be warm enough during the day to sit outside in December, but the nights will be cold. January and February are usually the coldest months.

Using the telephone & sending a letter

All telephone numbers in Aveyron contain ten digits and begin **05 65**. So, for example, calling the *Office de Tourisme* in Rodez, you would have to dial **05 65** 75 55 50. But if you are telephoning from abroad you need to add the international code for France which is **00 33**. When calling from abroad, however, you must drop the zero before the 5. So this time contacting the *Office de Tourisme* in Rodez you must dial **00 33 5** 65 75 55 50.

Addressing a letter in or to Aveyron is simple but requires that you use the appropriate postcode. All postcodes in Aveyron begin with the number **12** which is the number of the department - this can also be seen on the number plates of cars registered in the department. To write to the *Office de Tourisme* in Rodez, you use the postcode **12005** in the address, which is laid out as follows:

Office de Tourisme
6, place Jean-Jaurès
12005 RODEZ
France

Places to Stay

There are probably four kinds of accommodation which will interest the independent traveller most - hotel, *gîte*, camp site and *chambre d'hôte* - but there is also the increasingly popular *Village de Vacances.* All types of accommodation are well represented in Aveyron and all, generally, are very reasonably priced even during the main months of the summer tourist season. If you decide on a particular venue, it is always advisable to book in advance. But if you are more easy going about your holiday, wishing to leave as much to circumstance as to preparation, then you'll always find somewhere to stay, though obviously it will take a little longer and involve you in more adventure.

But whatever your planning, finding the spot that is perfect for you is as much a matter of luck as it is of research. So always try to be flexible and keep your eyes open, as Aveyron offers a range of potentially perfect stopping places in a variety of settings, from river valley to bastide town, from high mountain to meadow.

Hotels

Hotels are the most expensive sort of accommodation, as you will not only have to pay for your room but, unless you picnic, all your meals as well. Apart from a few hotels, usually ones with Michelin starred restaurants, most hotels in Aveyron offer good value for money. If you are selecting from a distance, you can consult hotel guides or contact hotels directly to answer any queries you have (preferably in French as otherwise you may not get an answer) or try the local tourist offices or even contact the French

Government Tourist Office in London.

When you arrive at a hotel, and if you are not so desperate you would sleep anywhere, then always trust your own judgement about whether it is the sort of place you want to spend the night. Check the location, the general state of repair, the reception area, assess the type of reception you get, but above all have a look at your room. Of course, this is a usual procedure in French hotels and not to do so will indicate a level of uninterest and may lead to you being accommodated accordingly.

French hotels charge per room and not per person so always check the price of the room before agreeing to book. If your French isn't very good, the cost of the room is always displayed in the reception area and on the inside of the bedroom door, where you can double check. You will probably be asked if you want breakfast, this means that it is not included and will cost you extra. Breakfast is the unexciting side of French cuisine, so don't expect the hotel version to set your palate alight first thing in the morning. Often you are better advised to look for a nearby cafe-bar, where it will be cheaper and probably better. A hotel may charge a disproportionally high price for such a simple meal.

There are some hotel suggestions at the end of each of the three sections - the North, the Centre and the South. Otherwise you can check:

The red **Michelin Guide** on Hotels and Restaurants.

The **Logis de France** Annual Guide.

The **Charming Small Hotel Guides: Southern France**

Or contact the local the *Office de Tourisme* in the area you are visiting for details of a range of accommodation. For **Logis de France** in Aveyron call or write to

Logis de France de l'Aveyron
Chambre de Commerce et d'Industrie
10, place de la Cité
12033 RODEZ
France

Tel. 05 65 77 77 04

Gîtes Ruraux

The *gîte* holiday offers one of the most popular ways to stay in the area. It has the advantage of providing good accommodation for the whole family at a reasonable price, and further allowing you to keep the overall costs down by preparing your own meals. The disadvantage is that you are confined to a single location for the duration of your stay.

Gîtes are basically country cottages, though they do include houses in smaller towns, especially picturesque ones such as Najac. Most of the cottages are owned by French people who rent their properties through French organisations such as Gîtes de France and Cléconfort or directly through local *Offices de Tourisme* and *Syndicats d'Initiative*.

British companies are gradually increasing their interest in the area. Many such companies are advertised in British newspapers, especially on Sunday, as are many privately owned British properties.

To contact the **Gîte de France** reservation service in Aveyron telephone:

05 65 75 55 55
or fax.
05 65 75 55 89

or write to

6, place Jean-Jaurès
BP 831
12008 RODEZ Cedex
France

Or to contact **Gîtes de France** in the UK write or telephone:

Gites de France
21/24 Grosvenor Place
London SW1 7HU

Tel. 0891 244123

Or to contact **Cléconfort** write or telephone

Association Meublés Cléconfort
Aveyron
33, avenue Victor-Hugo
12000 RODEZ
France

Tel. 05 65 73 63 27
fax. 05 65 73 63 29

Camping and Caravaning

The opportunities for camping in Aveyron are extensive and range from basic and very cheap *camping à la ferme*, where you are in close proximity to the farm and the farming community, to quite luxurious four star campsites, either municipally or privately owned. Sites are sometimes part of a chain, such as **Castels et Camping Caravaning** or **Sites et Paysages de France**.

Camping is a serious business and communes are willing to put up quite large sums of money to establish a camp site in their area. The business also depends on a large degree of return trade so care will be taken to make sure you are comfortable and have what you need. Campsites are well organised and you are advised to book in advance if you wish to make sure of getting the one you choose. If you don't mind where you stay or want to move around, you'll find a site somewhere nearby, even in summer.

The bigger campsites are usually in beautiful areas, offering a blend of natural, unspoiled environment and organised activities, such as watersports or horseriding. Most campers in Aveyron will be French as the French still holiday extensively in their own country and are more comfortable organising their own holidays than people in other European countries and the United States. You don't see many travel agents in France.

The Syndicat d'Initiative in Rodez will provide you with a brochure of campsites in Aveyron. An excellent range of recommended sites in France is covered in Alan Roger's book, **Good Camp's Guide: France**. His guide also contains adverts for companies offering to make advance bookings (ferries and campsites) for you.

Chambres d'Hôtes

The *chambre d'hôte* is the French equivalent of bed and breakfast. These are found in country areas and offer an interesting alternative to a night in a hotel. They are becoming increasingly popular in Aveyron and as more holidaymakers use them more are springing up.

Although the quality cannot always be guaranteed, the experience you will gain from this proximity to country life will, at very least, be interesting. The opportunity to spend a night or two in someone's house or farm is a rich one and of sharing their table and their company. If you are lucky you will enjoy a comfortable night's sleep after a well cooked meal in good company.

You can find *chambres d'hôtes* advertised at the sides of roads or, if you want to examine the alternatives, the tourist offices and *syndicat d'initiative* can supply you with a full list of what is available in the locality.

For information contact:

By phone 05 65 75 55 55

By fax   05 65 75 55 89

Village de Vacances

Halfway between a *gîte* and a campsite, the *village de vacances* is becoming increasingly popular in Aveyron for both French and foreign holidaymakers, especially families. There are about 20 in the department and they are to be found in lovely scenic locations in the countryside or by rivers, such as the Lot, the Aveyron and the Tarn, and offer quality chalet accommodation. There are often pools and tennis courts. The Office de Tourisme will advise you of their locations and booking procedures.

Here is a selection of villages de vacances from throughout the region:	
Aubrac	Le Royal Aubrac 12470 (05 65 44 28 41)
Belmont-sur-Rance	Le Seriguet 12370 (05 65 99 96 14)
Brommat	Village de Vacances 12600 (05 65 66 70 00)
Camares	Château de Camares 12360 (05 65 99 59 36)

Village de Vacance

Espalion	Village de Vacances 12500 (05 65 44 02 15)
Najac	Residence de Vacance Valvac 12270 (05 65 29 74 31)
	Villages Vacances Familles 12270 (05 65 29 73 97)
Nant	Relais Soleil 12230 (05 65 58 46 00)
Pont-de-Salars	Vacances Pour Tous 12290 (05 65 46 83 08)
Requista	Le Châ teau de Lincou 12170 (05 65 74 00 37)
Riviere-sur-Tarn	Peyrelade 12640 (05 65 59 80 74)
Rodez	Club Aquarius au Domaine de Combelles 12000 (05 65 77 30 04)
St-Jean-de-Bruel	Le Hameau du Viala 12230 (05 65 62 11 28)
Salles-la-Source	Village de Vacances de Pont-les-Bains (05 65 71 39 00)
Sauveterre	Les Chalets de la Gazonne 12800 (05 65 72 02 46)
Villefranche-de-Rouergue	Centre de Vacances Domaine de Lauriere 12200 (05 65 45 09 51)

Note that because of the 'secret' status of Aveyron or its simple invisibility, most holiday brochures printed in English do not market the department as a distinct area. Often it will be included in South West France, Midi-Pyrénées or even the Auvergne or the Cevennes. So to find out what is on offer in the area may often require persistence mixed with a bit of detective work.

Eating Out

As in other parts of France, eating out in Aveyron is a pleasure and, usually, not an expensive one. Many menus offer a range of dishes which reflect the region (South West France) and are prepared from good local produce. There are, however, many restaurants which specialise in the *menu de terroire*, offering the customer a variety of specifically Aveyronais dishes. The *menu de terroire* is not a gimmick to entice the tourist as these restaurants trade all the year round and so must take care of the quality and authenticity of their catering to ensure they maintain their local custom.

The *menu bourgeois*, which has enjoyed such a resurgence in Paris and is at the heart of French cookery, is widely available also, offering its ever popular choices from *escargot* to *coq au vin*. There are an increasing number of foreign food restaurants, especially in the towns, which cater for expanding local tastes. And, of course, fast food restaurants are springing up, though the population of the department is too small to attract much interest from the fast food giants. MacDonald's franchises have recently arrived on the busy roads around Rodez- though generally, like much else in Aveyron, fast food remains very much the product of local whim and enterprise.

Choosing a restaurant

When you eat in a French restaurant, and not an ethnic one or a fast food bar, the custom is you have the table for the evening or for the lunchtime. And the French regard for food is such that the meal will be long and evenly paced and you will not be expected, even if you are able, to gobble it down and leave. Food to the French is much more than a mere necessity and the time taken in devouring it offers not only the opportunity to satisfy your appetite in a sociable environment but the sensual exploration and evaluation of the art of tasting. In short, if you eat out expect to spend time doing it.

Choosing a restaurant is as much a matter of personal choice as it is one of being able to decode all the obvious signs of quality. High prices, a big menu and spotless, bright interior are no guarantee of a great dining experience. Outside of the Michelin starred restaurants, you should not have to pay high prices to enjoy a good meal. And high prices in Aveyron are nothing like the ones charged in London, New York or even Paris. And don't be fooled by the *menu gastronomique* into thinking you are getting better food than is on the ordinary menu. *Menu gastronomique* does not mean better food but more food and unless you are very hungry, forget it. It is a device to get the tourist to spend more money, you won't see locals going for it.

There are a few signs to look for, however. A full restaurant generally means a popular restaurant which translates as good food and good value. This does not always work because sometimes restaurants don't fill up till later and could only be half full at the time you decide to eat. But unless it is very early in the evening or else you are starving hungry avoid an empty restaurant. After twelve o'clock noon, always avoid an empty restaurant - if locals don't eat there, stay away.

A large menu displayed on the door or window showing off a long list of dishes is not a testament to the quality and versatility of the chef but more likely a guarantee that somewhere at the back of the kitchen there is a large deep freeze where your scallops or lobster thermidore have languished on cryonic hold. On the other hand, a hand written card or menu board advertising the *plat du jour* or the *menu du jour* will usually signify that the dish or dishes have been prepared for that day's meal.

An impeccable interior may be superficially attractive but remember that you do not feast with your eyes. A more used and lived in interior may indicate more customers and a greater concentration on the products of the kitchen than the impact of the surroundings. Of course, in the more expensive restaurants you'll probably get both, but then you've paid for it.

So when choosing a restaurant check the menus, for both type of food and the number of dishes; how many other people are eating there, it could mean the difference between a quiet night or one packed with noisy atmosphere; and look at the interior to see if it's really the sort of place you want to sit for an evening no matter how good the food is. And, finally and very importantly, check what the aromas coming from the kitchen are like. Are they filled with fresh, distinct and appetising promise or are they dull, blurred and as tired as the tastes they foretell? Good eating, after all, is about the eyes, the nose and the taste buds synchronised in perfect harmony.

Menus

From the menu you can either choose to eat *a la carte* or choose one of the set menus (*menu conseille* or *menu à prix fixe*) on offer - usually a restaurant will have more than one set menu. To choose to eat *à la carte* will give more choice but involve you in expense if you select more than the single dish. Look at the menu and you will see this, where the cost of a main dish is nearly equivalent to an entire set menu.

So take care if you're trying to budget you're spending on food. Set menus offer a good value meal where each course contributes to the overall eating experience, in terms of taste and satisfaction. So don't expect a single course from a set menu to be filling on its own but like instruments in an orchestra together they create the music.

Although eating out is usually a leisurely experience, more and more restaurants in towns are offering the alternative of a *menu rapide* for those whose time may be pressing.

Unless otherwise indicated, coffee and drinks cost extra and can make the bill mount up disconcertingly. So what at a glance seems a good value meal may end up not to be so.

Wines

Wine can add to the expense of a meal and in restaurants often costs only very little less that you would expect to pay in the UK or USA. Restauranteurs blame it on the tax they have to pay, but that is their story.

Some menus include wine in the cost of the meal. But don't expect quality, this is usually a *vin de table* and, at lunchtime especially, is supplied in generous quantity. Where it is included this is indicated on the menu as *vin compris* or *boisson comprise*.

When it comes to selecting from the wine list, use your common sense, balancing cost, what you are eating and you're mood for a heavy or light drink. Ask for advice, especially about local wines which are described in the later section on food and drink.

Mealtimes

Lunch is still a popular meal in France and in Aveyron from noon till two the restaurants are full of working people. A simple set menu lunch is good value but often concentrates more on bulk than finesse. Many country restaurants do their main or only trade at midday. Wine is usually included in the cost of these meals which allow for little if any choice - usually of colour only.

If your lunch requirements are more complex, then there are restaurants in the towns offering greater variety. If they are simpler, then most bars and cafes have a range of reasonably priced snacks. But if you want to be independent, try the *charcuteries* (delicatessens) and *pâtisseries* which have a wide range of perfect food for a picnic and visit a *cave* or *épicerie* (grocer's) for a bottle of wine to wash it down with. **Don't forget to do your shopping before twelve o'clock because after that time the shops will be shut for lunch.**

Reservations

It pays to make a reservation if you are eating out in the evening. If the restaurant is busy, you will certainly need to make one - an evening can easily be spoiled if you are made to wait or turned away. Making a reservation can help a restaurant as much as it helps you, as it allows the staff to pace the evening to ensure that each table enjoys good service. If you are asked to arrive at eight when you wanted to eat at seven thirty or vice versa, it is because other diners will be arriving at that time and the restaurant wants to ensure that everyone isn't expecting their meals at the same time.

Tipping

The cost of your meal and your drinks by law includes a 15% service charge, so you are neither obligated nor expected to give a tip. If, however, you feel the service was very good, you can show your appreciation by leaving a small extra sum for the waiter. But don't tip ordinary or merely satisfactory service as this gives the wrong message.

The NORTH

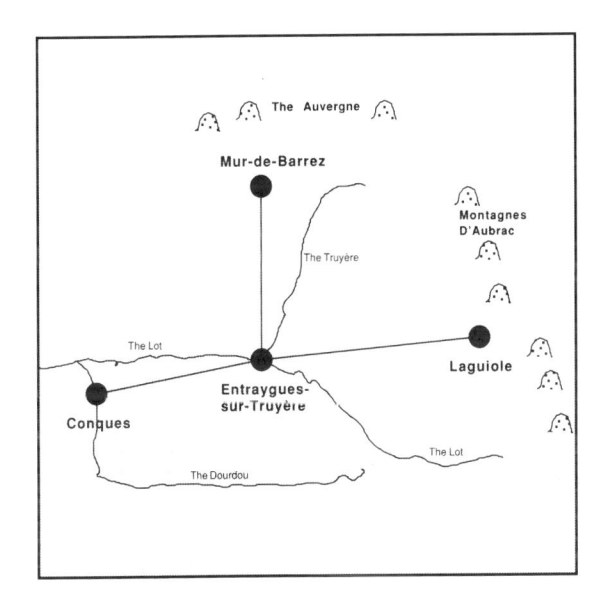

Map showing Mur-de-Barrez, The Auvergne, Montagnes D'Aubrac, The Truyère, The Lot, Laguiole, Entraygues-sur-Truyère, Conques, The Dourdou

In this section

Le Carladez-the far north,
The Montagnes d'Aubrac, the Lakes and the Truyère,
The Pays d'Olt (The Upper Lot Valley)
Between Entraygues-sur-Truyère and Conques,
South and West of Conques
Hotel and Camping Suggestions

The North

The northern-most tip of this part of Aveyron, known officially as *le Carladez* and locally as *le Barrez*, is where the foothills of the Auvergne descend to the valley of the River Truyère.

Here, both the landscape and the architecture feel as if they belong to the neighbouring department of Cantal. The land closest to the border rises to over a thousand feet and the isolated farm buildings are of low construction with steep roofs to combat the fiercest winds, rain and snow. Even Carladez's most famous son, Jean Verdier, who became Archbishop of Paris in 1929 and who dearly loved his birthplace, was reputed to have claimed that it had ' six months winter and twelve months bad weather'. A bit extreme, perhaps, but he makes his point.

The highest land in the whole of Aveyron runs along the North's eastern border and is called the **Montagnes d'Aubrac**. Even if the region lacks the truly mountainous, rocky Puys of the Auvergne, it does have dramatic sometimes wooded, often desolate landscape which has been likened to the Highlands of Scotland and Connemara in Ireland. Here the famous honey coloured cattle are brought up to the summer pastures between 25th May and 13th October. The first snows of winter fall in November followed by well over a hundred days of freezing weather. Unsurprisingly, the Aubrac is gaining a reputation for its ski stations and winter sports.

With the exception of these areas of high ground, the majority of northern Aveyron enjoys a much warmer climate where vines are grown in the sheltered valleys around the Lot and Dourdou rivers. Most of the small centres of population have grown up along the sides of these waterways. Some of the most charming are beside the Lot in a long, narrow region which crosses the whole department called the Pays

---

The highest point in Aveyron is in the Aubrac (1439m).

The lowest is in the Lot Valley (144m).

d'Olt, between the St-Laurent-d'Olt and Entraygues-sur-Truyère at the confluence of the Lot and the Truyère.

Another lovely area of hills and valleys is the Rougier de Marcillac and the startling red-stoned villages of the wine growing region. Though, undoubtedly, the most exquisite examples of fine mediaeval architecture and craftsmanship in this locality are to be discovered in Conques, ancient stopping place for pilgrims on their long journey to Santiago de Compostella.

In very sharp contrast, towards the western border, are four towns which owe their existence to the more recent industrial history of the last century. Aubin, Cransac and Decazeville once employed thousands of men in their mines and Capdenac-Gare was selected as the site for a crucial junction at the height of the development of the steam train. With the decline of both industries, the towns remain as monuments to their former affluence and importance.

The North

Over 220,000 hectares of Aveyron are covered in forest.

Espalion

Le Carladez
the far north

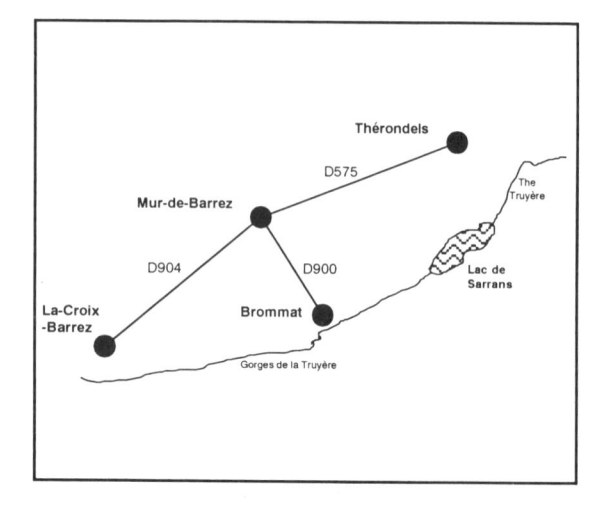

Mur-de-Barrez

(85K N of Rodez)

This capital town of Carladez is built on a volcanic outcrop at the end of a plateau which has magnificent views over the Bromme valley. Splendidly sited at the top of a steep climb through the town's side streets and up flights of stone steps are the boundaries of the twelfth century château. The whole place suffered in the past from attacks by the English, the Calvinists and the Huguenots, but much remains from previous centuries. A good deal of care and money has been spent over recent years in the renovation of the town's private and public buildings, presenting today's visitors with a centre of charm and taste. Of particular historical interest are the ruins of the château, the

Sunset on the River Lot

River Lot

Entraygues

Mur-de-Barrez

Conques

Conques

Gothic style church of St Thomas (named after Thomas à Beckett, who was patron of the parish) places celebrating the Grimaldis of Monaco who saved Mur-de-Barrez from being razed to the ground on the orders of Richelieu in 1620 - the **place de Monaco**, the **tour de Monaco** and even the **café de Monaco**.

Like nearby Conques, the town was a stopping place for pilgrims en route to Santiago de Compostella. Nowadays its visitors are right to have it on their itinerary of interesting Aveyron towns, perhaps making a special note to go on a Sunday morning when in Summer there is an outdoor market selling, amongst other things, examples of attractive basket work from the region.

The town has a variety of small cafés and restaurants serving regional dishes but for a snack try a local speciality from the patisserie called a tarte à l'encalat - a sweet pastry base with a kind of junket centre flavoured with orange flower water. Like many other cakes and pastries of the region, it won't be the most exciting thing you've ever eaten, but it is authentic, very much a creation of the limited local produce.

Market day:
Thursday

Information:
Office de Tourisme,
12 Grand Rue 12600
tel. 05 65 66 10 16
fax. 05 65 66 06 02

Thérondels

(10K N E of Mur-de-Barrez)
During the last century thousands of Aveyron's inhabitants left the department to seek a new life in Paris. In order to retain their identity, they formed an association in the capital and returned to villages of their birth for celebrations each year. More recently many have bought or built second homes in Aveyron. Such is the case in Thérondels, where the original village has expanded to encompass new Parision owned houses.

It is certainly a lovely area for summer holidays, being close to the Auvergne to the north and within easy reach of the beautiful, peaceful Lacs de Sarrans on the Truyère to the south.

The old village has an eleventh century church, solid grey stone houses and a central square with magnificent lime trees. The **hôtel-restaurant Miquel** is worth a visit and there is a four star campsite.

Brommat

(3K SE of Mur-de-Barrez)
Since barrages were constructed across the Truyère by the EDF, creating attractive new stretches of water, the area around Brommat and the Lac de Sarrans has become very popular with French and foreign tourists. The municipal campsite, with its good facilities and pleasant locations, attracts an increasing number of people each year.

Lacroix-Barrez

(19 K NNE of Entraygues-sur-Truyère)
The village prides itself on being the birthplace of Cardinal Verdier, archbishop of Paris, son of the local blacksmith-come-innkeeper. A statue of Jean Verdier stands in the square and his life and achievements are to be found in the crypt of the church, which he had had built in 1932.

Lacroix-Barrez is in a beautiful area of wooded hillsides between the gorges of the Goul and the Truyère. It's an excellent place for walking in the countryside or exploring the tiny villages and hamlets, such as Valon (formerly Avalon), Madrière and the ancient Roman site of **Bars.** There is a small municipal campsite and a hotel-restaurant, **Le Commerce.**

The Montagnes d'Aubrac, the Lakes and the Truyère

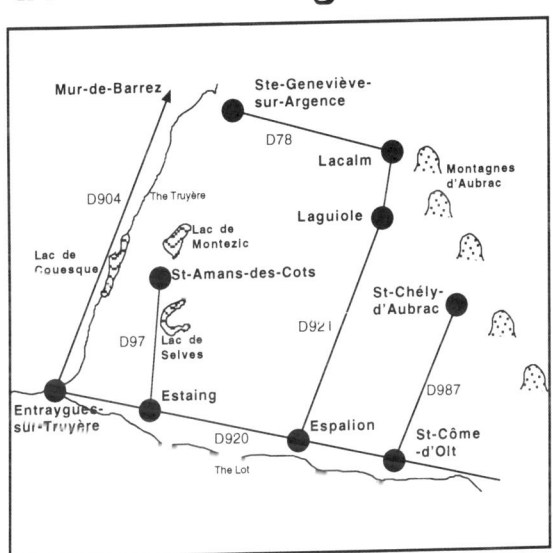

Sainte-Geneviève-sur-Argence

(24K NNW of Laguiole)

The Lac Sarrans and the Truyère River separate Mur-de-Barrez from Ste-Geneviève-sur-Argence built on two facing hillsides each at a height of 200 metres above the river valley. The town makes a pleasant stopping place and the restaurant at the Hôtel de Voyageurs does very reasonably priced meals, including regional specialities.

Market day: Wednesday

Information:
Syndicat d'Initiative
Mairie 12420
tel. 05 65 66 41 16

The River Argence is well known in the area for its trout fishing. Its source is in the Aubrac where it is called the Argence la Vive. Shortly after Ste Geneviève, it is joined by its grimly named partner, the Argence Morte.

Lacalm

(10K N of Laguiole)

This village has always been a popular stopping place for travellers, having a hotel and several café-restaurants, and being situated on the main D921 from Espalion to Laguiole.

Since the Aubrac began to welcome more winter skiers and summer holiday makers, small places like Lacalm have to varying degrees offered facilities to the new visitors. From the hotel or municipal campsite people go on foot, by bike or car to explore the Aubrac, the river valley of the Truyère, the nearby lakes and the countryside around.

Lacalm itself has some interesting old buildings, including an eleventh century church with its original vaulted ceiling. If you come across the name Clairon Rolland in the village, it's the nickname of the local postman who, in the mid nineteenth century, was the bugler attached to a battalion fighting in Algeria. Apparently, during the battle of Sidi Brahim when French forces were under seige, he sounded the attack rather than retreat for which he gained renown, though the subesequent conflict was lost with 22 Aveyronais dead. He had to wait a long time, however, for this and other acts of heroism to be recognised. He was 93 when finally honoured by the then president of the French republic, Poincaré.

Lacalm is the highest village in Aveyron.

Cassuéjouls

(6K NNW of Laguiole)
One nearby 'paradise' to visit, especially at lunchtime, is this tiny village which locals will convince you was created by God himself.

Apparently, on the evening of the sixth day of creation, God told the archangel Gabriel that He wanted to reserve a pretty corner on earth where he could go and rest from time to time. So Gabriel went off and eventually found a beautiful valley with a sparkling stream surrounded by hills. God was so pleased that He personally put the finishing touches to it - the two stone bridges (one basalt, one granite), beech woods and a spring with water possessing curative powers. He'd just completed this work and was just about to take a break, when news began to reach him of the downfall of Adam and Eve. So angry was He that He decided to leave Earth for ever and set off down the road to Laguiole. (I'm not sure what this tells us about Laguiole!)

Who knows, you may travel to Cassuéjouls along the same road! Once in the village park near the church and the village green, and the village's one restaurant, Chez Collette, which is very popular with locals and serves a moderately priced lunch of good regional dishes.

To get to the spring water (which is recommended as a cure for a whole list of ailments from ill temper to anaemia) follow the signs through the village, over the stream and along an unmade road for a short walk in the country. If it's a hot day you'll probably be thirsty by the time you get there, but do take your own drink with you just in case the distinctive taste of rusty nails is not to your liking!

The North

Laguiole

(55k NNE of Rodez, 25k NNE of Espalion)

Laguiole (pronounced La - yol), the capital town of the Aubrac, is famous today for its knives and gastronomy. As a place of architectural interest, only the old streets leading up the hill to the **church of St Mathieu** are of any significance. This is a remnant of the old town which, like many in the region, suffered from attacks by the English in the fourteenth century, when its fort was destroyed.

The more modern main streets and some of the side alleys boast a proliferation of knife shops, knife museums, knife exhibitions, gift shops (with knives) and restaurants (with knives.... and forks!). The largest knife in town is in the Allée de l' Amical in Honore Durand's establishment; it weighs 192 kilograms and is 3.54 metres long. In case you are in any doubt as to the main industry of the town an 18 metre high knife blade, designed by Philippe Starck, points provocatively to the sky from the roof of the knife factory as you leave the town.

> **Information:**
> Office de Tourisme,
> place du l' Ancien
> Foirail 12210
> tel. 05 65 44 35 94
> fax. 05 65 54 10 29

Since 1947, the market place has been presided over by an enormous bronze Aubrac bull - work of the sculptor, Guyot. The real Laguiole cows, which are led to the high pastures of Aubrac in summer, returning to the warmer lower slopes in winter, give milk for the cheeses produced at the cooperative Jeune Montagne, one of which, the tome fraîche, is the main ingredient in the aligot of the Aubrac region. (See **Food and Drink** section) The town is also home to some interesting charcuterie - sausages (fresh and dry), hams, tripeau of sheep's giblets and sheep's stomach, stuffed with veal, ham and Aubrac herbs.

One of the most famous fouaces, a regional cake of exceeding dryness (see **Food and Drink** section), is made by the Roux family business to a recipe handed down through five generations. Such was its appeal tha Cardinal Verdier, the only Archbishop of Paris from Aveyron, ordered one a week to be made for him in a local pâtisserie in the capital.

If you want to dine well and in opulent style, there are a couple of very good places to eat in town, but if you want a really gastronomic experience book a table at **Michel Bras' Restaurant** on the route de l'Aubrac, open from April to October. He's been described as a 'cuisinier-poète'; certainly, his fascination with the Aubrac, which he regards as his 'garden', has resulted in an innovative menu of excellence. He claims to...'capture the smells, the sounds, the winds. I play with the elements. My cooking is born of the sky, the earth, the water..... it strives to reinterpret the countryside. It is the expression of the Aubrac with which one cannot cheat, as one does not cheat with nature.' His creations are said to appeal to seven senses - sight, touch, smell, hearing, taste, soul and pleasure!

Irresistible?

The North

Market day: Saturday

Aubrac and Saint Chély d' Aubrac

(18K NE of Espalion)
These two villages are excellent centres for exploring this desolate but magnificent region of Aveyron. For very keen walkers who are looking for a challenging holiday on foot, there is a circular route called the **Grande Route (GR) Tour de l'Aubrac** which goes from Aubrac to Laguiole and then up and across the **Montagne d'Aubrac** and into the next departments of Cantal and Lozère and back.

For those preferring an afternoon walk, it's possible to

park in Aubrac itself and walk along part of the Tour d'Aubrac to the highest viewing point in Aveyron, the **Truques d'Aubrac**, where there are spectacular views across the Montagnes and the causses. You can also visit **Belvezet** or **Bonnefou-d'Aubrac**, close by, if you want to take any panoramic pictures.

St Chély d'Aubrac is a peaceful, charming, historic village with a fourteenth century church, a central square with cafes and parking and quiet little streets.

Both Aubrac and St Chély d'Aubrac were significant stopping places for pilgrims in the Middle Ages. Apart from the physical hardship of the journey across the high, often barren landscape, the travellers were also in danger from highway robbers and must have been relieved to reach the safety and hospitality of such places. The roads and crosses littered about the area amply testify to the pilgrims' presence.

An example of an early hostelry is the **Domerie d'Aubrac,** just below St Chély, built on the orders of a Flemish pilgrim in the early twelfth century. Enduring robbery on his outward journey to Santiago de Compostella and a blizzard on his return, he saw to the construction of the Domerie on the site of his dual survival, just below St Chély d'Aubrac.

If you happen to be in the area on the Sunday nearest 25th May, you will witness (along with thousands of others) the **Fête de la transhumance** when cattle are brought up from the sheltered, warmer valleys to the high summer pastures.

For an ancient and authentic experience, (and it is wise to book in advance) head for one of the remaining *burons* where laguiole cheese is made. At some, during the summer, you can sit outside the old stone buildings at tables under the trees and sample the home-produced *aligot* - a local dish of potatoes,

---

Information:
Syndicat d'Initiative,
Mairie 12470
tel. 05 65 44 21 25
fax. 05 65 44 20 10

cheese and garlic. The word *aligot* comes from the Latin and means 'a little something to eat', originally made from bread and cheese the modern day version with potato is certainly much more than 'a little something', so don't snack before hand. There are two such *burons* near St Chély d'Aubrac called **Calmejane** (near la Croix des Trois-Eveques) and **Canuc** (by the D219).

Castelnau-de-Mandailles

(12K E of Espalion)
This extended commune is said to have its toes in the river and its head in the clouds. The lower half, Mondailles, is really one long street from the church to the ancient chateau ruins. It's near a lovely spot on the Lot River by the lake created by the construction of the **Barrage de Castelnau-Lassouts**.

The upper part, Castelnau, is an ancient village, once completely fortified, which retains some wonderful old houses and an eleventh century church. From the nearby **puech des Condamines** and **Puy de Barry** (both over 800 metres high), there are excellent views.

Keen walkers may note that they can join the **Grande Route 65** just north west of Castelnau and walk about 15K up to the highest point in the Aubrac. There are two local walks (*sentiers de petite randonnée*) which can be enjoyed as well or instead, called *Le Cerf* and *Lou Duganel*.

Saint-Amans-des-Cots and the Lakes

(20K N of Estaing, 20K W of Laguiole)
Saint-Amans is at the centre of an area which has become increasingly popular for tourists and local visitors since the electricity company, EDF, constructed barrages damming the small rivers to create a number of man-made lakes. It is an ideal holiday centre with excellent camp sites, beautiful scenery and opportunities for numerous sports and activities, including water skiing, boating, tennis, golf and horseriding. Near the most easterly lake, the **Lac de Galens**, is an attractive stopping place for those energetic walkers following the **Grande Route 416** which winds east to Laguiole and north to Sainte-Geneviève-sur-Argence.

There are no other towns of any significant size in this region and you'd have to go to Entraygues or Estaing to find a hotel, but Saint-Amans-des-Cots and the lakes of **Montézic, Couesque, Maury, Selves** and **Galens** would each make a delightful venue or a peaceful centre for a camping holiday.

Market day: Thursday

Le Nayrac

(9K N of Estaing)
In recognition of the care and hard work lavished on the houses both ancient and modern and the expertise of the inhabitants in flower growing, this village has justifiably been awarded the top prize for floral villages in Aveyron. Even one of the two hotel-restaurants has renamed itself the *Auberge Fleurie*! At the height of its floral splendour, Le Nayrac presents a superb array of colour against the grey granite of its old buildings.

Saint-Symphorien-de-Thénières

(12K NW of Laguiole)
The tiny village lies north east of the lovely **Lac de Montezic** and a couple of kilometres to the west are the **Gorges de la Truyère**. This sheltered area at the foot of the Montagnes d'Aubrac is ideal for camping. There is an excellent four star site at the edge of the lake called *Camping Municipal de Saint-Gervais*.

The village of Saint-Symphorien-de-Thénières was the object of an attack by the English during the Hundred Years War when the church was partially destroyed. It was rebuilt in the fifteenth century and houses some interesting stone sculptures. From the ruins of the château de Thénières on a granite outcrop north of the village, there are good views of the surrounding countryside.

The Pays d'Olt
(The Upper Lot Valley)

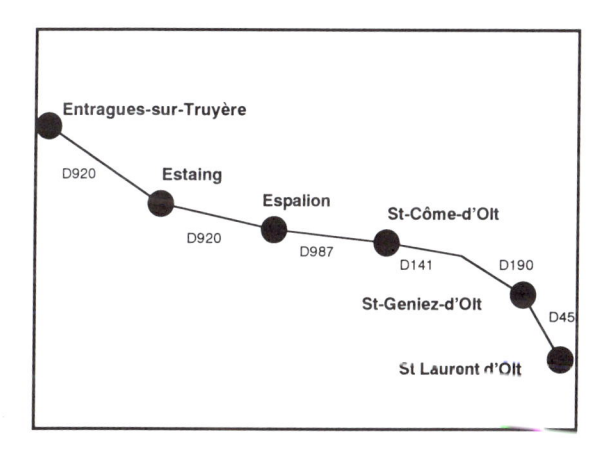

```
Entragues-sur-Truyère
    D920
        Estaing
            D920    Espalion
                    D987    St-Côme-d'Olt
                            D141    D190
                                St-Geniez-d'Olt
                                        D45
                                    St Laurent d'Olt
```

One of the most picturesque areas of northern Aveyron follows the windings of the River Lot from Saint-Laurent-d'Olt to Entraygues where the Truyère joins the main river. This long thin area of land and waterway extends across from the north eastern almost to the north western borders of the department. It is known by its Celtic name, the Pays d'Olt. Here, the deep river valley offers protection from the cold winds of the high Aubrac and the region has an appreciably warmer, gentler climate.

Saint-Laurent-d'Olt

(12K E of Saint-Geniez-d'Olt)
The village is within a kilometre of the Aveyron boundary, at a point on the Lot where the river valley is narrow, sandwiched between the foothills of the Aubrac to the north and the Causses of Séverac and Sauveterre to the south. The village itself is about fifty metres above a meander in the river, its highest point being its thirteenth century château which was rebuilt in the eighteenth - a time when the village was at its most prosperous, producing *Cadis*, a light woollen serge cloth.

If you are interested in literature written in the old *langue d'Oc* (which is still spoken and indeed is being revived in the department) then visit the **Musée Jean Boudou** for insights into the life and writings of the most respected modern *ecrivain occitan*. (If you want to visit the tiny village where he lived (1920 - 1975), **Crospin** is to be found in the Ségala region, south west of Rodez and Baraqueville, between the town of Naucelle and the River Viaur on the D58.)

If you wish to stay here, there are three hotel-restaurants and a campsite.

Saint-Geniez-d'Olt

(4K E of Espalion)
This small town, built on both sides of the river, was once the second most important in the old region of Rouergue. Originally, it was a small mediaeval village on the right bank where you will still find some wonderful examples of timber framed houses with overhanging top storeys.

Then in the seventeenth and eighteenth centuries three industries were established (nail-making, tanning and cloth-making) which resulted in a second half being built on the left bank and the population increasing to over five thousand. At the height of its success some splendid hotels and houses were constructed and in the **hôtel de ville**'s *Salle des Illustres* you'll see portraits of the town's most prestigious citizens of the period.

There are two large campsites (one four star, one two star) and several hotels with restaurants as well as other cafes and bar-restaurants. If you're in the town in the early summer, you're sure to be offered strawberries everywhere, for the *fraise de Saint Geniez* replaced the grape as a major crop in the vicinity when the vines were destroyed by phylloxera and by the 1850s a thousand tonnes were being produced. Unfortunately, with early import from Spain, the demand has dropped and the cooperative now sells about eighty tonnes a year.

Market day:
Saturday
(Strawberry fair in May)

Information:
Office de Tourisme,
4 rue du Cours 12130
tel. 05 65 70 43 42
fax. 05 65 70 47 05

Sainte-Eulalie-d'Olt

(25K SE of Espalion)
Although the village is tiny, it is a popular place for lunch during the summer months, especially with fishermen and families who've spent the morning

✳
Plus beau village de France

> Information
> Office de Tourisme
> 05 65 70 43 42

further downstream on the **Lac de Castelnau**. Many people also choose Sainte-Eulalie as a holiday centre, staying in one of the small hotels or on the municipal camping site.

If you want a birdseye view of the River Lot or to take a memorable photograph of the area, make your way up to the **Puy de Campech** (nearly 900 metres high) which is an extinct volcano and proffers a panorama of the river below and the *causses* to the south.

Saint-Côme-d'Olt

(4K E of Espalion)
This is one of the most beautiful and well presented mediaeval small towns in the area. You pass into the old town through one of its three ancient gateways and enter into a living museum of stone houses, narrow side alleys built off the main streets which lead to the **château des Castelnau** at the centre. It was restored in the fifteenth century and now houses the *mairie*.

�֍
Plus beau village de France

There are two churches in Saint-Côme. The older, to the north, was built in the eleventh century but was superceded in the early fifteen hundreds by a wonderfully flamboyant Gothic church built on the orders of Antoine d'Estaing, the prior of Saint-Côme and bishop of Angoulème. The most stylish and unique feature is the bell tower which dominates the skyline like a section stolen from the corner of a fairytale castle.

> **Market day:**
> Saturday
> (summer only)

> Information
> Syndicat d'Initiative
> 05 65 48 24 46

The town offers good places to stay and eat and there is a municipal campsite called the **Belle Rive**, open from May to September.

Espalion

(31K NE of Rodez)

Four times the size of its near neighbour, Saint-Côme, Espalion is a busy market town offering the visitor a good selection of shops, eating places, hotels, riverside stalls, museums and exhibitions. The most picturesque area is undoubtedly by the **Vieux Pont,** now used only by pedestrians, and built in the thirteenth century of warm red local stone. Most of the tall buildings flanking the river have enviable wooden balconies adorned with red geraniums in the summer months.

One way you can enter Espalion is from Rodez, down a steep road, passing by the ruins of the town's ancient château on the hilltop which was aptly described by the playwright, Antonin Artaud as hanging from the sky like ancient teeth. From Laguiole you'll enter from the north over the **Pont-Neuf,** built in the nineteenth century. Or, of course, you may arrive at the town from the east or west along the Lot Valley. These four approaches are, historically and geographically, the reason for the town's existence and continuing importance in the region. (It had, in fact, the status of *sous-préfecture* for over a hundred years.)

It is still a well frequented shopping centre as well as a popular place to break a long journey or stay for a holiday in one of its hotels or large municipal campsite, the **Roc de l'Arche**. It's also a good place to stop for a meal. The restaurant at the **hôtel Moderne** has gained a high reputation in Aveyron, especially for its excellent fish dishes.

Information:
Office de Tourisme,
2 rue Saint-Antoine
12500
tel. 05 65 44 10 63
fax 05 65 48 02 57

Market day:
Monday, Friday

Estaing

(7K NE of Espalion, 38K N of Rodez, 42K E of Conques)
Estaing is tucked into a bend in the river at the bottom of a wooded hillside. At the top of the small town is its extraordinary château, begun in the thirteenth century, restored in the fifteenth and sixteenth and seemingly added to and altered by each succeeding generation. The resulting architectural jigsaw is quite unique! And it's open to the public.

Information:
Syndicat d'Initiative, Mairie, rue Francois-d'Estaing 12190
tel. 05 65 44 03 22
(open 15 June - 15 September only)

It was at Estaing that those on pilgrimage to Santiago de Compostella crossed the Lot over the arched Gothic stone bridge. Present day tourists frequently choose the town for a day trip (there are several good eating places) or to stay in its hotels or campsites. (There are two campsites - the larger, la **Chatellerie**, is open all year round; the other, the **Hauterive**, opens from June to September only.)

✻
Plus beau village de France

Visitors to Estaing should definitely succumb to the temptation of the local *vin d'Estaing*. It is authentic and interesting and can only be bought in the region, since it is produced in comparitively small quantities each year. (See **Food and Drink** section.)

Collectors of interesting jewellery might like to look out for *la croix du Pont d'Estaing* which is produced in plain gold or decorated with precious stone

Golinhac

(5K SSE of Entraygues)
The village overlooks the Lot from an elevated site on the left bank. Its ancient houses which were built on granite with slate roofs have been well renovated. Its chateau, however, has fallen into complete ruin.

It used to be a stopping place for pilgrims. Now it offers *gîtes ruraux* in the nearby hamlet of **Balledou**. There is also a small municipal campsite.

Entraygues-sur-Truyère

(55K N of Rodez)
Although its full name suggests it's on one river, the derivation of *Entraygues* reveals a truer picture. The word comes from the Latin *inter-aquas,* between waters. The waters in question are the Truyère and the Lot which converge at this point.

For hundreds of years the river provided the major form of transport for produce of the area - charcoal, wood, fruit and vegetables and the wines of Entraygues and le Fel. Now the boating is purely for pleasure and sport, and the rivers continue to provide excellent venues for fishing.

Off the main road which runs through the town there are fascinating little streets, courtyards and passageways with houses of varying styles from the fifteenth to the seventeenth century. The original château belonging to the counts of Rodez suffered extensive damage by fire and was rebuilt in 1654.

This is a truly delightful place to stop on a sunny day, to walk by the rivers and enjoy a picnic or a meal in one of the town's bars or restaurants. There are four hotels, but most people who come here for a holiday choose to stay on one of the campsites. The largest, a municipal site called **Val-de-Saures,** has 250 places and offers good facilities. **Camping Ronque Pailhol** has only 66. Both are open from June to September.

Market day:
Tuesday, Friday

Information:
Office de Tourisme,
Tour-de-Ville 12140
tel. 05 65 44 56 10

Enguialès

(5K W of Entraygues-sur-Truyère)
After Entraygues, the Lot makes an almost ninety degree turn to the west. The D107 follows the river from Entraygues and for the first five kilometres there will be turnings off to the right (north) to the commune known as Enguialès. The largest centre of population in the commune is **Le Fel**, which boasts a hotel, three restaurants and one remaining tower of its chateau. The prime reason for its fame, however, is the limited production of local Le Fel wines. A few bottles find their way to the vintners of Villefranche de Rouergue. A close second is the **cabecou du Fel**, a local cheese which is eaten fresh or preserved. (See **Food and Drink** section.)

Between Entraygues-sur-Truyére & Conques

Sénergues and Espeyrac

(9K E of Conques) and (3K E of Sénergues)
The most straightforward way to go from Conques to Entraygues-sur-Truyère and the Pays d'Olt is to follow the D107 up the Lot valley. The most challenging route, however, is a tiny road (the D42) from Conques which winds its mainly single tracked way through some beautiful countryside and two small villages - Sénergues and Esperac. These little historic hideaways have become quite popular centres for summer holidaymakers, especially cyclists and walkers. There are two hotel-restaurants in each village and a four star campsite with 60 places in Sénergues. Many people who stay here are tempted

to follow in the footsteps of the ancient pilgrims who walked across this region from Conques towards Estaing in the Pays d'Olt. Now, there is a clearly signed section of the joining the two towns.

Both Sénergues and Esperac have well maintained old buildings, many (like Sénergues' fourteenth century church) are constructed of granite. Esperac's main claim to historic fame is that it was the birthplace of a blind man called Guibert who miraculously regained his sight thanks to the healing power of Sainte Foy's relics in Conques.

South & West of Conques

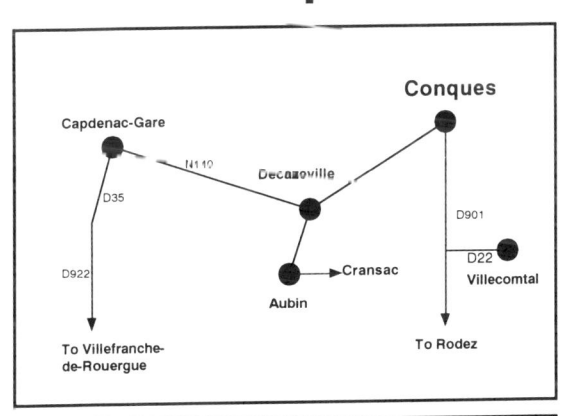

Conques

(38K NNW of Rodez)
Whether you discover Conques up the steep climb from the valley road north of Rodez or glimpse it first from the surrounding hillsides at **Combes, Bancarel** or **Cendie,** you will without doubt be enchanted by the exquisite mediaeval village. The name derives

from the Latin *concha* meaning shell, which aptly describes the geological shape of the immediate landscape, where the **gorge of the Ouche,** previously narrow and steeply wooded, widens out into a softer more open aspect before the river meets the **Dourdou,** west of Conques.

Throughout its history, Conques has been a place of spiritual significance. The earliest Christian settlement was destroyed by the Saracens in AD 730, then reinstated by Pepin le Bref and Charlemagne to shelter the hermit, Dadon. Soon a community of Benedictines was established, living in comparative obscurity and poverty until a monk named Ariviscus, with an eye to the main chance and a blind eye to the eighth commandment, brought the stolen relics of Sainte Foy (a 12 year old martyr from Agen) to the abbey. From that moment on miraculous cures occurred, the most famous being a blind man, Guibert, who recovered his sight in AD 980.

In the eleventh century, Conques prospered as one of the more important stopping places for the pilgrims on route to Compostella. At this time, the church itself was built, between AD 1041 and 1099. By 1300 there were over 3,000 inhabitants. This period of popularity and riches lasted for about 300 years after which the monastery fell into decline until, by the beginning of the 1400s there were only 29 monks left. The neglected buildings suffered further at the hands of the protestants and later the revolutionaries. It was only Prosper Mérimée, novelist, dramatist and *inspector général des monuments historiques* under Napoleon III, who saved Conques from complete devastation in the nineteenth century.

Since then both the religious edifices and the picturesque houses have undergone meticulous restoration, preserving for the modern pilgrim, the tourist (3000 a year!), a living museum with a strong spiritual centre.

The North

There are over 4,000K of rivers and streams in Aveyron.

✳
Plus beau village de France

In July and August, Conques is very busy, but somehow the crowds never seem to spoil the unique charm of the place. Perhaps this is to do with the terraced nature of the town built up the steep hillside with its warren of tiny streets, miniature gardens tucked in hidden corners and its three dimensional jigsaw of irregular roofs whose rounded slates have the irridescence and overlapping patterns of glistening fish scales.

You will find, at any time of year, that most people congregate around the **Abbatiale Sainte-Foy** in the heart of Conques. Above the church's main door is an extraordinary tympanum depicting Christ in the centre of the scene of Judgement flanked by the saved and the damned. Not only is it exquisitely carved, but it is most ingeniously positioned to catch the varying lights and shadows throughout the day which create a continuum of subtly changing images.

Inside the eleventh century church, the ancient original craftsmanship in stone and wood has been most carefully lit by natural light coming through the new windows, designed by Pierre Soulages who spent seven years painstakingly trying, rejecting and finally choosing what he knew to be exactly the right glass to create the effect he had envisaged.

Information:
Office de Tourisme, place de l'Abbatiale 12320 tel. 05 65 72 85 00 fax. 05 65 72 87 03

The first *trésor de Conques* is a collection of religious works of art and craftsmanship which have had special significance for the worshippers for a thousand years. The oldest exhibit dates from the ninth century, the most recent from the thirteenth (a silver plated figure of the Virgin Mary). But the most famous is a superb statue of Sainte Foy seated on a throne. The original figure was carved in wood then covered in gold leaf and studded with precious stones.

The second collection of artefacts and furniture

dating from the sixteenth and seventeenth centuries is to be found in the same building as the Syndicat d'initiative where you can find out about the numerous events organised in Conques and the surrounding area, including a film festival during the summer.

If you're feeling energetic, its well worth taking one of the walks up the opposite hillside of **Bancarel**. From here, in perfect peace and serenity, you can look back to the mediaeval jewel of Conques in its steep wooded setting and perhaps, when you've recovered your breath, appreciate in some measure the experience of the early pilgrims.

Saint-Cyprien-sur Dourdou

(7K S of Conques)
This village has, because of its location near the **Gorges du Dourdou**, has become much used as a camping centre. It's easily found on the D901 Conques to Rodez road and offers the visitor an excellent centre for exploring the Marcillac wine growing area and seeing the religious and architectural treasures of Conques itself. For shopping, Aveyron's capital city, Rodez, is a little over 25K to the south.

Every August there is a *fête des Parisiens* to celebrate the return of the Saint-Cypriens who left (or whose forbears left) Aveyron to seek work in Paris.

The village has its own version of the *fouace* (a cake flavoured with orange flower water) made to a family recipe in the patisserie in the **place des Forains**.

Auzits

(10K SE of Decazeville)
The village, situated on a wonderful elevated site, was once the commanding location occupied by the Chevaliers of Malta and had a monastery, hospital and a château. Later, many inhabitants were employed in the mining industry at Aubin and Decazeville to the north.

Today, it's a good area for walking and horseriding and visitors can get a good, inexpensive meal at the **Relais du Château**.

Cransac

(3K E of Aubin)
At the height of the industrial success of mining the Decazeville - Aubin - Cransac triangle, there were over seven thousand inhabitants in this 'new town'. Now there are barely two thousand and Cransac has lost its industrial 'look'.

The town may have lost its mines, but its other natural resource has now come to the fore as an attraction for local people and those from further afield. It's secret to success is, in occitaine, its *Puech que ard* (burning mountain). This phenomenon produces dry hot gases of up to 280 degrees centigrade which provide the heat necessary to support the thermal spa. Between April and October over two thousand people seek treatment, many for rheumatism in the steam rooms.

There are several good hotels, restaurants, a campsite and a variety of shops in the town which has plenty of green spaces and activities for children.

Information:
Office de Tourisme,
1 place Jean-Jaurès
12110
tel. 05 65 63 06 80

Aubin

(4K S of Decazeville)
At one time Aubin was the local capital, but it was superceded when the neighbouring mining town of **Decazeville** became the principal centre of population and influence.

Unlike Decazeville, which really superimposed itself on the little village of **La Salle**, Aubin retains some vestiges of its pre-industrial age. A simple square tower is all that remains of the old castle belonging to the Counts of Rodez. There is a tenth century chapel (restored in the nineteenth) and the twelfth century church of **Notre Dame de l'Assomption**, In the old town there are streets of ancient houses, some with timber frames, leading up to the old fort.

If the mining industry interests you, you can visit the **Musée de la Mine** whose entrance imitates the opening to a real mine. Inside there are industrial scenes, documents, tools and film shows. A guided tour will take about an hour. It is open every day from June until September from 10 - 12 am and 3 - 6pm.

Market day
Wednesday, Friday

Information:
Syndicat d'Initiative,
place Jean-Jaurès
12110
tel. 05 65 63 19 16

Decazeville

(39K NE of Villefranche-de-Rouergue)
Present day Decazeville has half the population it had in the 1830s when the original town, called La Salle, was engulfed by the thousands of buildings constructed to house the hoards of men who had newly arrived to work in the coal mines. This 'new' industry was the brainchild of the duc Decazes, a minister in the government of Louis XVIII, who created the Society of Coal mining and Foundries in Aveyron in 1826. The new mining town which grew up as a result was named after him.

The mining and smelting industry had a chequered history, faring badly against its rival, Aubin, which won the battle for the railway link. Later problems were the blueprint for the horrors of Zola's 'Germinal'. They resulted in the army firing on the crowd, at one point, killing seventeen people, including two women and a child.

The actual open mine, *La Découverte*, is an extraordinary spectacle, resembling a roughly hewn amphitheatre with alternate black and white terraces revealing the stratas of coal and rock. If you want a guided tour, apply to the tourist office in the town.

Decazeville, being built comparatively recently, has an architecture unlike any other town in Aveyron. Its church has paintings of the stations of the cross by Gustave Moreau who, strangely, would only undertake the work on condition that they remained unsigned.

The town's museum - **le Musée régional de géologie** - in avenue Paul Ramadier presents a well documented exhibition of geology and mining. It is open only in July and August. Decazeville is perhaps best visited on a Tuesday or Friday when the excellent open air markets take place.

As a footnote, it is worth recording that it was miners from the town who were directly responsible for resurrecting wine growing in **Marcillac** and the **vallée de Vallon** after phylloxera had devastated the region in the nineteenth century. Many of the miners, recruited from the villages and towns of the vallée de Vallon, returned to their tradition of wine growing in their spare time, often working at nights by the light of their miners lamps, to raise a meagre vintage. This grew until Decazeville became the main market sustaining a healthy production of quaffable wines. In the 1960s, the closing of the mines meant that

The North

Market day:
Tuesday, Friday

Information:
Office de Tourisme,
square Jean Segalat
12300
tel. 05 65 43 18 36
fax. 05 65 43 19 89

Marcillac faced a second crisis, this time an economic not an agricultural one. They solved it in two ways, by improving quality and by expanding their market beyond the immediate region. But without the hard work, ingenuity and a deep-veined tradition enduring in a group of miners from Decazeville, this industry would not have survived at all.

Bouillac

(10K E of Capdenac-Gare)
At one time, Bouillac was a thriving river port taking coal from Aubin and Decazeville to Aquitaine. Now it's a lovely peaceful village with swimming and boating for summer visitors. It boasts the longest bridge across the Lot (150 metres), a well preserved fourteenth century château and an eighteenth century church, though, strangely, the most imposing structure is a pigeon house in the middle of a field at the edge of the village.

Livinhac-le-Haut

(5K NW of Decazeville)
Idyllically situated on the banks of the Lot, the village is a wonderfully peaceful place to stay or to visit for the day. Once the village traded with Bordeaux, now it sits quietly by a bend in the river, sheltered from behind by high wooded hillsides.

There's a small two star campsite, called **camping Beau-Rivage**, which has only twenty five spaces so advance booking is probably a good idea. It's open from mid- June. There you'll also find a hotel-restaurant called **Soulié.**

Flagnac

(6K N of Decazeville)
More elevated than Livinhac-le-Haut, and on the opposite side of the river, Flagnac is a pretty old village which from June to September offers camping and boating to its summer visitors. The ancient buildings in its main street have timber framed upper storeys, though the owners have chosen to plaster over most of them. Nevertheless, the place has charm and retains a sense of antiquity.

Capdenac-Gare

(23K N of Villefranche-de-Rouergue)
If you journey to Aveyron from Paris by train, your first stop in the department will be here. In fact the town only exists because when the railway was constructed in the 1850, a new administarative centre was part of the planning and the site chosen was a tiny hamlet, called Tinsou, by the Lot River. This became Capdenac-Gare, new sister town to **Capdenac-le-Haut** which is in the next department, Lot.

In its heyday the town thrived, but was also reliant on the trade of the railway administrative staff and that of the passengers from as many as forty two trains which stopped at the station each day. Unfortunately, the depot closed in 1961 causing inevitable unemployment and loss of trade.

Market day:
Tuesday (main market), Saturday

Information:
Office de Tourisme,
place du 14 juillet
12700
tel. 05 65 64 74 87
fax. 05 65 80 88 15

Hotels, restaurants & hotel - restarants of the North

- some suggestions -

Hotels/HotelRestaurants	Restaurants
(* denotes Hotel Restaurant)	
AUZITS 12390	
	Relais du Chateau
	(05 65 63 91 67)
CAPDENAC-GARE 12700	
Terminus	La Cave
(05 65 64 74 47)	(05 65 80 82 40)
Auberge de la Diege*	
(05 65 64 70 54)	
CASSUEJOULS 12210	
	Chez Collette
	(05 65 44 33 71
CONQUES 12320	
Auberge St-Jacques*	
Logis de France	
(05 65 72 86 36)	
Auberge du Pont Romain*	
(05 65 69 84 07)	
Hostellerie de l'Abbaye	
(05 65 72 80 30)	
Le Moulin de Cambelong*	
(05 65 72 84 77)	
Sainte-Foy*	
(05 65 69 84 03)	

Hotels/Hotel-Restaurants

CRANSAC12110
Le Coq Vert* Logis de France
(05 65 63 28 80)

Hostellerie du Rouergue*
Logis de France
(05 65 63 02 11)

du Parc* Logis de France
(05 65 63 01 78)

DECAZEVILLE 12300
Moderne*
(05 65 43 04 33)

De France*
(05 65 43 00 07

ENTRAYGUES 12140
du Centre
(05 65 44 51 19)

Le Lion d'Or*
(05 65 44 50 01)

ESPALION 12500
de France
(05 65 44 06 13)

Moderne, Logis de France
(05 65 44 05 11)

ESTAING 12190
aux Armes d'Estaing*
(05 65 44 70 02)

Le Manoir*
(05 65 44 70 10)

LACROIX-BARREZ 12600
du Commerce*
(05 65 66 03 04)

Restaurants

& L'Eau Vive
(05 65 44 05 11)

Le Pont Vieux
(05 65 44 01 95)

L'Auberge Saint Fleurie
(05 65 44 01 44)

Au Bel Horizon
(05 65 44 70 90)

Hotels/Hotel-Restaurants

LAGUIOLE 12210
L'Aubrac* Logis de France
(05 65 44 32 13)

Regis*
(05 65 44 30 05)

Le Laguiole
(05 65 48 48 81)

LE FEL 12140
L'Auberge du Fel*
(05 65 44 52 30)

MUR-DE-BARREZ 12600
Auberge du Barrez* Logis de France
(05 65 66 00 76)

ST-AMANS-DES-COTS 12460
Auberge de Cassou*
(05 65 44 84 76)

ST -CHELY-D'AUBRAC 12470
de la Vallee
(05 65 44 27 05)

ST-GENIEZ-D'OLT 12130
de France*
(05 65 70 42 20)

Le Lion d'Or* Logis de France
(05 65 47 43 32)

de la Poste*
(05 65 47 43 30)

STE-EULALIE-D'OLT 12130
Au Moulin d'Alexandre*
(05 65 47 45 85)

**STE-GENEVIEVE-
SUR-ARGENCE 12420**
de Voyageurs* Logis de France
(05 65 66 41 03)

THERONDELs 12600
Miqel*
(06 65 66 02 72)

Restaurants

Buron de Burgas
(05 65 48 45 80)

Au Petit Creux
(05 65 44 30 60)

Michel Bras*
(05 65 44 32 24)

Camping

CAPDENAC-GARE
Camping Municipal
(05 65 80 88 87)

CONQUES
Camping de l' Etang du Camp
(05 65 79 62 25)

CAMPING DU MOULIN
(05 65 72 87 28)

ENTRAGUES
Camping Municipal
(05 65 44 56 92)

ESPALION
Camping Municipal
(05 65 44 06 79)

ESTAING
Camping Municipal
(05 65 44 72 77)

LAGUIOLE
Camping Laromiguiere
(05 65 44 44 64)

MUR-DE-BARREZ
Camping de la Source
(05 65 66 05 62)

ST-AMANS-DES-COTS
Camping Municipal de Lavergne
(05 65 44 89 02)

ST-GENIEZ-D'OLT
Camping la Boissiere Campeoles
(05 65 70 40 43)

STE-EULALIE-D'OLT
Camping Brise du Lac
(05 65 47 55 55)

STE-GENEVIEVE-SUR-ARGENCE
Camping Municipal
(05 65 66 49 63)

The CENTRE

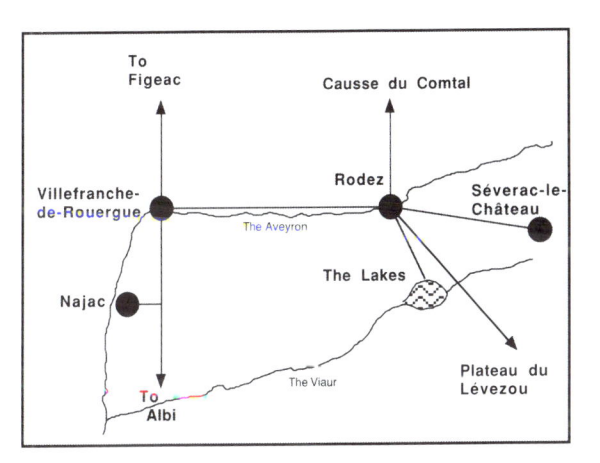

In this section

Villefranche-de-Rouergue
North West of Villefranche-de-Rouergue
North East of Villefranche-de-Rouergue
East of Villefranche-de-Rouergue
Najac
East of Najac
Rodez
West of Rodez
East of Rodez
Hotel and Camping Suggestions

Rodez, the Capital of Aveyron, is 643 kms. from Paris.

West of Rodez between the Aveyron and Viaur rivers is a region of soft and beautiful countryside, its patchwork of small fields often reminiscent of South Devon. It possesses high ridges, hidden valleys, thriving small towns, bastides, innumerable stone-built villages and hamlets - some well cared for others almost uninhabited and falling into ruin.

North of the D911 Villefranche-de-Rouergue to Baraqueville road are two river valleys the Alzou and the Aveyron. The latter, the more picturesque, winds its way from Rodez to Laguepie in Tarn et Garonne through some incredibly steep sided, wooded gorges crossed occasionally by the hairpin of a country road and dotted with a few pretty villages.

South of the D 911, lies the Ségala and an area which is veined by the tiny tributaries of the Viaur, known as 'the land of a hundred valleys'. Here, the small country roads and narrow lanes form a confusing network, but one well worth 'losing' yourself in.

Make sure you have the appropriate Série Bleue map, otherwise getting lost can be an all too literal experience.

Exploring these country lanes is important if you want to look into the heart and soul the region and understand the nature of the local temperament.

The western half of Central Aveyron is where the best examples of bastide towns are to be found. The expansive fortified grid of Villefranche's narrow streets is geometric in its precision around a central square of high colonaded buildings; while to the south, Najac clings gratefully to the back of an undulating, spiny hill; and further south again, Sauveterre, a bastide in miniature, is so beautiful and so perfectly maintained that going there is like straying into a meticulously crafted film set.

The Ségala which extends eastwards to join the plateau of Lévezou was, two hundred years ago, a very poor region where not much grew but chestnut trees and what little cultivation there was took place around tiny farms and hamlets in the valleys. It was an area where bandits preyed on travellers journeying between *baraques* (primitive inns offering protection and the solace of a basic bed and sparse meal). The inhabitants of Ségala were known as *ventres noirs* (black bellies) because of what they existed on, a near starvation diet of bread made mainly from rye and chestnuts.

In the last hundred years, a gradual revolution in the agriculture of the region has taken place. As a consequence, the people abandoned their valley houses for the once arid plateaux whose soil was quickly being enriched by lime and, later, chemical fertilisers brought into the region first by the railway (which was laid in 1902) and more recently by improved road links with the rest of France.

Positioned almost exactly in the centre of the department is its historical capital city, **Rodez,** strategically built on top of a rocky hill above the River Aveyron.The vine growing area of **Marcillac** with its pretty grey or red stone villages and its warm microclimate lies twenty five kilometres north of **Rodez.** North east, towards the foothills of the high Aubrac, is the **Causse du Comtal,** famous for its cattle and sheep rearing and equally renowned for its cheese production.

The **Causse de Sévérac**, about 50K east of Rodez, is the northernmost part of the **Parc Naturel Régional des Grandes Causse**. It is flanked by the River Aveyron to the south and its tributary, the Serre, in the north. It takes its name from the town of

The Centre

There are more dolmens in Aveyron than any other French department.

Séverac-le-Château whose oldest buildings date from the eleventh century. The region is forested and somewhat austere with high rocky outcrops or *puechs*, some of them over 900 metres in altitude, good for walkers with energy to burn.

To the south east of Rodez are the **Plateau du Lévezou** and the two large EDF lakes, the **Lac de Pont-de-Salars** and the **Lac de Pareloup**, fed respectively by the Viaur and the Vioulou rivers. Both are wonderful places for water sports, picnics and, of course, camping.

The Centre

Aveyron is the fifth largest department in France and the largest in the Midi-Pyrénées region.

Lunac church

Villefranche - de-Rouergue

Bastide- Royale

(55K W of Rodez)
Some 16K north of Villefranche-de Rouergue are the **Grottes de Foissac**, described as a 'veritable underground museum', which provide fascinating evidence of pre-Christian settlement in the area. Remains of Bronze and Iron Age life are mainly centred in the north and east of Aveyron, but the Gallic tribe, the Rutènes, inhabited the whole of the area covered by the department. They built some vast fortified settlements (*oppida*) as well as other, more commercial centres, focussing on exploiting local materials and metals, such as silver in Villefranche-de-Rouergue. This industry continued to thrive during the five centuries of Gallo-Roman civilisation.

At this time, the settlement was a small village called La Peyrade, on the left bank of the river Aveyron. It was expanded and renamed in 1099 by Raymond IV, Count of Toulouse. The rapid expansion of the town on the right bank was begun by the King's brother, Alphonse de Poitiers, who established power and influence in the area at Najac and then at Villefranche-de-Rouergue in 1252.

The new town was designed as a *bastide,* with its 4 *quartiers* of grid-like streets and central square surrounded by arcaded buildings. (See **Bastides.**) Opening on to this square is the main church of the town, dating from 1260, **la collégiale Notre Dame**. There are numerous other smaller churches and chapels, perhaps the most beautiful being the **Chapelle des Pénitants Noirs**, near the northern town wall, which dates from 1642 and was built by the

The Centre

brotherhood of Penitants Noirs of Villefranche, founded in 1609.

Across the river on the Najac/Cordes road is the **Chartreuse Saint-Sauveur**. This fifteenth century monastery has a magnificent square of cloisters (one of the largest in France with thirteen four roomed 'houses'), a *chapel des Etrangers* for pilgrims, a *Petit Cloitre* for the monks and a church whose choir stalls, like those in the town's collégiale Notre Dame, were sculpted by André Sulpice.

> **Information:**
> Office de Tourisme, Promenade du Giraudet 12200
> tel. 05 65 45 13 18
> fax. 05 65 45 55 58
> (Open all year)

If you have only one day to visit Villefranche-de-Rouergue then make it a Thursday. For Thursday is market day. From early morning until mid-day the whole place throbs with noisy life, both human and animal. In the **Place Notre Dame**, the ancient cobbled square surrounded by cool stone arcades, a slick vendor of kitchen gadgets keeps up a non-stop patter into his microphone, demonstrating the cutting and slicing of vegetables with the skill and sleight of hand of a card sharper. Further on, a little old lady, toothless, bent almost double, brown and wrinkled as a Agen prune, displays the basketful of home grown produce she has pushed to the market in a homemade, wooden trolley before you were even awake that morning. There are local cows' and goats' milk cheeses, herbs and spices, plants, fresh vegetables and succulent fruit, wine, honey and every conceivable part of a duck - from stuffed neck to bones for your soup.

If you prefer your chicken or duck in its precooked state and you're willing to walk through the streets with your purchase flapping in your hand then have a look in the **Place André Lescure** as well, there you can choose your bird large enough to eat or small enough to rear. Between October and December a poultry market is held in **la Halle**, a large glass-sided building at the back of the church of Notre Dame. Here there is a seasonal sale of 2.5 tonnes of duck

Villeneuve

Rodez

Lake near Pont-du-Salars

Villefranche

Belcastel

The square - Villeneuve

La Bastide l'Évêque

La Fouillade

livers, 400 kilos of goose livers, 10 tonnes of whole ducks, 15 tonnes of ducks with no livers and 3 tonnes of geese whose livers have been removed for the production of foie gras.

Beyond la Halle is the **Allée Aristide Briard**, a wide tree-lined street, closed to traffic on Thursday mornings to make way for clothes stalls (you wondered where the country women bought that little shapeless number for the summer - now you know!), butchers, charcutiers, more cheese sellers and even more vegetable stalls.

> **Market day:**
> Thursday
> (A Foire of walnuts and chestnuts is held on 4th Thursday in October)

During August, you'll also find a rather strange extension of the market in the **Boulevard Charles de Gaulle**; it's somewhere between an antiques fair and a car boot sale. You have a sneaking feeling it's there for the increasing number of tourists, though it does seem to attract a fair amount of local middle class interest as well.

So, is Villefranche worth visiting during the rest of the week? Most definitely. Without the market and the crowds you can appreciate the unique lay out of the bastide town - narrow cobbled streets spreading out geometrically in a right-angled grid from the central square to the boundary walls. Wonderful old houses with overhanging top storeys. Small shops, cafes and restaurants, churches, an ancient stone bridge over the river. And beyond the old boundary there's all the usual variety of out-of-town shopping which attracts people from a wide area in Aveyron - hypermarkets, DIY stores, garden centres, electrical goods and furniture stores.

At twelve o'clock, all offices, businesses and most shops will shut and those working in them will head off for a leisurely two hour Aveyron lunch, either at home or at one of the town's many restaurants. At lunchtime in Summer and on market days car parking spaces are at a premium, so plan in advance, by the time your stomach tells you it's time to eat it may be already too late to park.

Close by are a number of other interesting places. 2K to the west of the town off the Montauban road is the sixteenth century **Château de Graves**. Along the same road, 5K to the west of the town, is the **Parc aux Oiseaux** which has one hundred and fifty species of birds and some farm animals. It is open 10am - 7pm from April to September and midday - 7pm from October to December.

North West of Villefranche -de- Rouergue

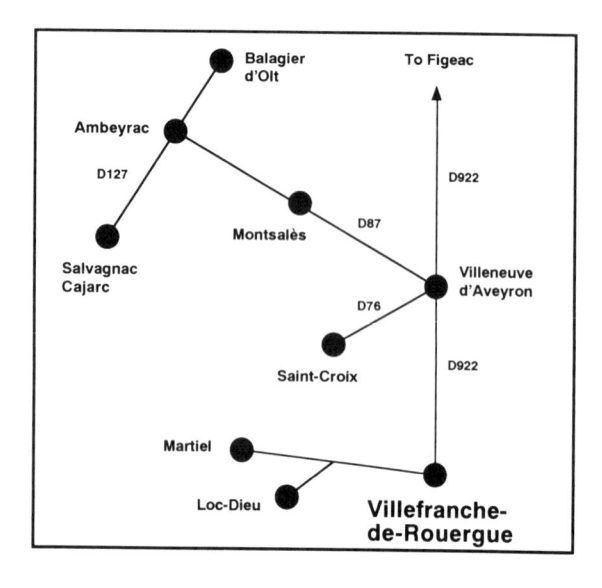

Savignac and Loc-Dieu

(3K W of Villefranche-de-Rouergue)
These are two places to visit to the west of Villefranche-de-Rouergeu off the D926. Savignac, which has really become a dormitory for its *bastide* neighbour, retains some remnants of its historic past in its church, fountain and one tower of its former castle. It also has a restaurant, **La Glebe**.

The more spectacular is the Abbey of Loc-Dieu which is used occasionally for classical music and choral concerts. (The *Office de Tourisme* in Villefranche-de-Rouergue carries details of the programme.) The abbey is in a superb parkland setting and is currently owned by the Montalivet family. There are guided tours in July and August from 10 - 12 am and 2 - 6.30 pm (not Tuesdays), though it is possible to arrange visits at other times of the year. (Again ask at the *Office de Tourisme.*)

Martiel

(6K W of Villefranche-de-Rouergue)
Just off the Villefranche-de-Rouergue / Cahors road (the D911) is this little haven of tranquility with its tree-lined square and its restaurant, **La Cazelle**, named after the many stone shepherds' huts in the locality. The nearby woods of Margues are excellent for walking and over thirty dolmens are hidden somewhere in amongst the trees! Only two of them are actually signposted.

Sainte-Croix

(8K NW of Villfranche-de-Rouergue)
This has been the site of human habitation since

prehistoric times. Today, you can see some fourteenth century houses and dine at either of the village's two restaurants, the **Ortalo** or **Chez Jean-Louis Ausset**.

Its busiest time of the year is the last Sunday in August when there is an evening banquet serving the village's famous *poule farcie* to over 700 guests. This offers a great opportunity to experience a past custom which still has life today.

Montsalès

(16K NNW of Villefranche-de-Rouergue)
This tiny village once had a château constructed in 1260 and later extended. Only its fourteenth century tower remains standing near the church. On the way down to the Ambeyrac road is a large wash-house, known as the **Lavoir de Brignoles**, with stone pillars supporting its roof. Also in the vicinity are the **dolmen de l'Homme Mort** and the **grotte de la Gleio de Maou** where a neolithic site was dicovered in the last century.

Salvagnac-Cajarc

(25K NW of Villefranche-de-Rouergue)
This most westerly village in Aveyron is in an idyllic setting on the south bank of the River Lot. It is literally joined to its twin, Cajarc, in the next department (Lot) by a suspension bridge. The village has some lovely narrow ancient streets, a fourteenth century castle built on a rocky spur and a church which was once the castle's chapel. It also has, nearby, the **Roc d'Anglars** from which a peasant girl, deserted and forgotten by her royal lover leapt in her grief from the rock into the fountain below where she drowned. A happier local connection is that this was the holiday area enjoyed by former French President George

Pompidou who owned a property just across the river!

Ambeyrac

(17K NNW of Villefranche-de-Rouergue)
Another small village, just southwest of Balaguier d'Olt, which has seen the height and passing of its major trade. Previously, like many other parts of Aveyron, this was an area for growing rye. Much of it was used to make the famous straw hats of Tarn-et-Garonne and, before the manufacture of the modern plastic alternative, its hollow stems were also used for drinking straws. Now, strangely, a very successful home industry has grown up in the village since the early nineties when Maryse Cepière set up her workshop creating fashion items for women which are sold in Paris and abroad.

Balaguier d'Olt

(22K NNW of Villefranche-de-Rouergue)
At one time this pretty little village on the Lot was a riverside port trading with Bordeaux in wine and hemp. It has many charming houses, some with wooden balconies, which are built overlooking the river on the rocky cliff from which two streams pour into the river. It's a picturesque place to visit for a view of the valley and to lunch at the **restaurant La Grange**.

If you're in this area, you may wish to stop for lunch at the **restaurant de la Source** and then go on to neighbouring **Camboulon,** a most attractive, mainly mediaeval village.

North East of Villefranche-de-Rouergue

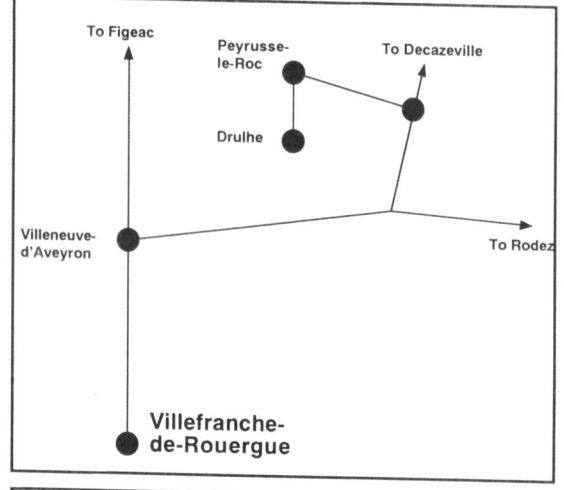

Villeneuve

(11K N of Villefranche-de-Rouergue)

Of the bastide towns of the Rouergue, the one with the oldest and most interesting history is Villeneuve-d'Aveyron. Unlike the other four (Najac, Villefranche-de-Rouergue, Bastide-l'Evêque and Sauveterre), this bastide was constructed around already existing buildings.

The beginnings of Villeneuve date back to 1053 when Odile de Morton, inspired by his pilgrimage to the Holy Land and with the authorisation of the Bishop of Rodez, built a church and monastery modelled on the St-Sepulchre of Jerusalem. In the twelfth century, two

---

Information:
Syndicat d'Initiative,
place des Conques,
12260
tel. 05 65 81 79 61
(Open May until end of October)

gateways were constructed called the **Porte Issaurenque** and the **Porte Manhanenque**.

The bastide town, with its formal planning of streets round a central square, surrounded by high walls, was the brainchild of the Count de Toulouse, Raymond VII, who also extended the original church and gave the inhabitants of the town their freedom in 1231. In 1249, following the death of Raymond VII, Villeneuve passed into the hands of Alphonse de Poitiers, brother of King Louis, and became a *bastide royale* in 1272.

The final piece of construction in this era was as a result of the declaration of war against the English, when, to complete the town's defenses in 1343, the Tower de Cardaillac was built.

Visitors to Villeneuve today will find a beautifully restored and maintained little town, with cafes, restaurants, shops, cool stone arcades around the central **Place des Conques** and historic buildings. In the church is a wonderful fresco from the fourteenth century of a pilgrim on his way to Santiago de Compostella who could have stopped straight out of the pages of Chaucer's 'Canterbury Tales'.

During the summer there are dances and dinners organised in the town when local participants dress in mediaeval costume. For these and many other local events the town's *Syndicat D'Initiative* is helpful with up to the minute information and advice.

Drulhe and Peyrusse-le-Roc

(42K NNE of Villefranche-de-Rouergue)
North East of Villeneuve and Villefranche-de-Rouergue, two of Aveyron's most beautiful bastide

towns, are two villages which retain fascinating, evocative remnants of bygone ages.

Information:
Syndicat d'Initiative, Mairie, Peyrusse-le-Roc 12220
tel. 05 65 80 42 98

Drulhe was an ancient command post of the Templars before it was taken over at the end of the fourteenth century by the Hospitaliers of St Jean de Jerusalem. From this period there are still remaining a twelfth century tower and a mediaeval well, which is set against the wall of the restored church where the imprints of the buckets and ropes used by villagers over the centuries can be clearly seen.

More spectacular by far is the site of **Peyrusse-le-Roc**, once a thriving wealthy settlement in the Middle Ages with its castle, church, synagogue, a maladerie for lepers, a covered market, village houses (some with columned facades and wooden balconies) and a fourteenth century cross of St George. This fortified village owed its prosperity to rich mineral deposits of silver, lead and antimony which were mined nearby.

Today, the inhabited part of the village is being carefully restored and has a peaceful charm of its own. Beyond the walls you can walk down to the ruins where you are faced by the most breathtaking view of the **Roc del Taluc**, a precarious granite outcrop on which is balanced the square towered remains of the lower château. If you have a good head for heights, you can ascend the stone steps and enjoy an incredible view over the valley and the **Adierne stream**.

Two other square stone towers, the **Porte de Barbacane** and **le Beffroi**, form part of the ancient ramparts. Unlike any other mediaeval site in this part of Aveyron, Peyrusse-le-Roc more closely resembles a Cathar fortress and possesses a similar strange magic.

Montbazens

(27K NE of Villefranche-de-Rouergue)

Montbazens and Rignac to the southeast are the two main markets for the sale of animals reared in the area - pigs, sheep and cattle. It is in this region that the farmers decided to promote their veal calves as being reared naturally with their mothers. (A sign you'll see on most of the veal sold in Aveyron butchers.)

> **Information:**
> Syndicatd'Initiative,
> Mairie 12220
> tel. 05 65 63 77 94

The little town has been justifiably recognised as achieving a harmonious mixture of old and new buildings using local materials which blend perfectly. It has also for some years been a centre for countryside holidays with activities and entertainment organised and run within the commune.

East of Villefranche-de-Rouergue

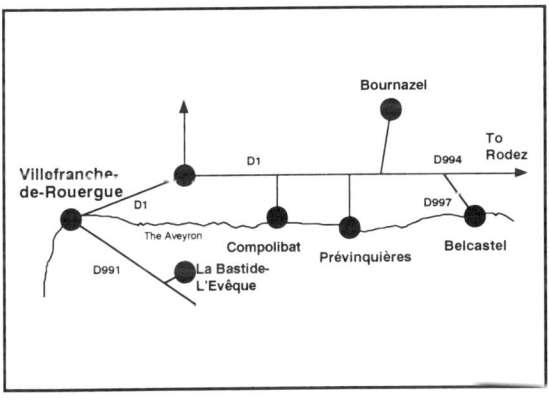

La Bastide-L'Evêque

(10K E of Villefranche-de-Rouergue)

Information:
Syndicat d'Initiative,
Mairie 12200
tel. 05 65 29 93 01

This rural commune was founded in 1280 by Raymond de Calmont; the bishop of Rodez. Unfortunately, little remains of the original bastide which was fortified in the fifteenth century. There is evidence of the streets built at right angles to each other, a couple of old wells and a few ancient houses, but the most impressive building is the fourteenth century church. This is a solid stone edifice with simple gothic interior features.

La Bastide-L'Evêque is a lovely peaceful rural centre for a holiday, within easy reach of Villefranche-de-Rouergue and Najac. It offers hotel, *gîte, chambres d'hôtes* and *camping à la ferme*.

You can buy local food such as *foie gras*, *confit*, *pâtés* and fresh produce at the farm, **la Bastide Gourmande**. At the Chambert-Mazars' farm, **la ferme de Cruorgues**, between 4 and 6 o'clock on a Friday, you can obtain home made cheeses - the rest of the time they spend at the markets in the area, where you can also buy their produce.

Compolibat and Prévinquières

(20K E of Villefranche-de-Rouergue)

Information:
Syndicat d'Initiative,
Compolibat, LeBourg
12350
tel. 05 65 81 95 50

A very pretty section of the footpath, the **Grande Route 62B** (which runs along the Aveyron valley from Villefranche-de-Rouergue to Rodez), is located between these two villages. Though it does get steep in places.

Compolibat is on the right bank of the river at the

bottom of the valley in a snug area of chestnut woods. It comprises just one street but does have somewhere you can stop off and eat. Upriver can be found the curious result of erosion known as the **Igues.**

Prévinquières overlooks the Gorges d'Aveyron from the left bank. It is a lovely little spot with narrow streets and attractive sixteenth century houses.

Belcastel

(23K E of Villefranche-de-Rouergue, 19K W of Rodez)
From the castle on top of a steep rocky valley, the village houses spill down the hillside to the Aveyron where an ancient stone hump-backed bridge spans the river. It is an absolutely delightful spot. A picture postcard maker's dream of heaven. Where ever you look there are beautifully restored timber framed houses with grey roofs and pretty terraced gardens. The zigzag streets are cobbled, offering at each turn wonderful views of the valley below, the wooded hillsides and the old church, hotel and idyllic little campsite on the other side of the river. The *Office de Tourisme* has booklets of quite challenging local walks and information about the village's history. For a less strenuous stroll, walk down river to the **Grotte du Loudon** and across the wooden bridge and back to the village on the other side.

On Sunday lunchtime especially, there is an incredible buzz of conversation from the very popular restaurants which attract diners from the locality as well as many tourists in the summer months. The most expensive, but gastronomically superb, is the **Vieux Pont** which has built up an excellent reputation for Nicole Fagegaltier's award winning cuisine. The restaurant **Coudorc le 1909** offers very good local menus at reasonable prices.

The Centre

Information:
Office de Tourisme
12390
tel. 05 65 64 46 11
Open June until September

※
Plus beau village de France

Bournazel

(28K NE of Villefranche-de-Rouergue)
The village is quite charming and has been improved by having its square and some of its streets newly paved. But the main reason to visit is to see one of the most beautiful Renaissance castles in Aveyron.

Najac

Bastide Town

(24K S of Villefranche-de-Rouergue)
There many reasons why Najac has become the focal point for tourists in the summer months. First, it is incredibly beautiful: the bastide town and its dominant castle overlook one of the most scenic parts of the Aveyron valley. Just across the road from the new town, with its large car park, post office and gendarmerie, the old bastide stretches like a spine along the narrow, steep hill which juts into the path of the Aveyron river. A wide tree-lined street, flanked on the one side by cool stone arcades and on the other by a line of houses reminiscent of Tudor England, slopes gently down to the town square. What looks like an old fashioned band-stand on the right is where the machine used to be kept for the public weighing of the once famous local ham, *Jambon de Najac*, now only obtainable at Claude Barriere's. Each Sunday morning, a busy market takes place amid the atmosphere of this old square selling a variety of manufactured, crafted and fresh produce, including jewellery, clothes, baskets, hams, honey, wines, fruit, vegetables, delicious cooked chicken and freshly rendered duck fat - the traditional basis of cooking in the South West France.

Market day:
Sunday (summer only)

From the square a narrow, very steep street leads picturesquely down to the rest of the town before rising again steeply to the church and the castle, perched on their vantage over the river. The castle, higher and older of the two, dates back to the eleventh century, but was added to in the thirteenth century when the bastide town was constructed, like Villefranche-de-Rouergue, the brainchild of Alphonse de Poitiers. The **church of St Jean**, a squat building heavy in design and mood, has a rather unusual history - it was built by order of the Inquisition by the inhabitants of Najac by way of punishment for having embraced Catharism which may account for its lack of earthly transcendence.

In the Aveyron valley below the town is an excellent camp site by the river and a small holiday village with chalet accommodation and an outdoor swimming pool for public use. (Men note, only swimming briefs are allowed not swimming trunks - this can lead to misunderstanding if you do not go prepared!). The campsite is tastefully hidden in the trees beside the river but the chalets of the holiday village are obtrusive when you view them form the town.

Over the old bridge you'll find the **Belle-Rive hotel and restaurant** (which serves a very good local cuisine) which also has a swimming pool for the use of clients. To the right of the bridge a single car roadway leads to one of the tiniest stations in the area. Waiting for the night sleeper to Paris at eleven pm, looking up at the stars and the illuminated castle, which seems to be floating high above you in the firmament, is an awesome experience!

In spite of being very busy in the summer months, this is a delightful centre for a holiday. As well as the very good camp site, there are hotels of various prices and pleasant *gîtes* to hire. The river valley offers good relaxed canoeing, but make sure you

※
Plus beau village de France

The Centre

Information
Office de Tourisme, place du Faubourg
12270
tel. 05 65 29 72 05
fax. 05 65 29 72 29

book in advance and check that the river has enough water to make it a canoeing excursion and not a walk in water. There are many excellent walks and pony trekking available.

There are several good places to eat: the **Belle Rive**, by the river; in the town there is **Oustal del Barry** which has a proven reputation and offers a high priced but good value Menu Gastronomique; also in the town is the popular **Il Cappello**, an inexpensive Italian restaurant which also offers some good local cuisine; and across the river on the hill opposite Najac is the **Cornaille** offering creative, good value cuisine in a country setting with spectacular views.

East of Najac

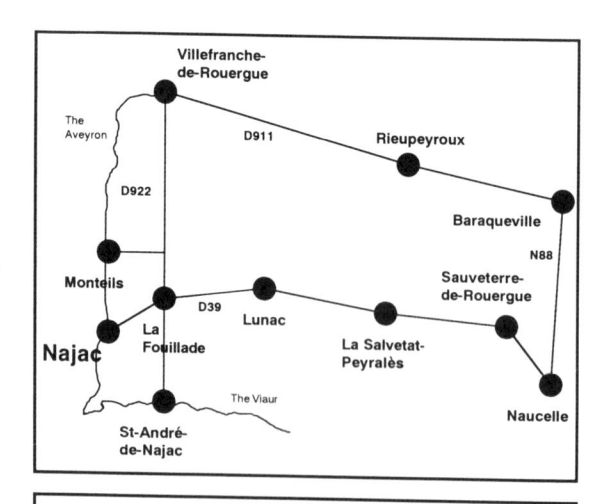

Monteils

(10K S of Villefranche-de-Rouergue, 7K N of Najac)
The village is in a lovely part of the Aveyron valley. It

is a popular place for camping in the summer months and is a good centre for walking, horse riding and sightseeing. Monteils has only a couple of streets around the church, a shop, bakery and some vestiges of its earlier fortifications. There are two restaurants, one belonging to the village's only hotel, which in its former life had a very different function! (Its attractions were advertised by a pair of bloomers waving from the tree outside.) A more recent commercial success is the farm owned by Jacques Carles which is widely promoted in the area for its production of foie gras, pates and duck. You'll get a very friendly welcome, an insight into the secrets of local cooking and a chance to sample a selection, washed down with a glass of good local wine. For a very much more expensive meal in a lovely setting, visit the splendour of **Longcol** up the winding, climbing road from Monteils on the road to La Fouillade. A former farmhouse, Longcol has been superbly restored and is unusually adorned inside with treasures from the East.

Information:
Syndicat d'Initiative,
Mairie 12200
tel. 05 65 29 63 48

Sanvensa

(9K S of Villefranche-de-Rouergue)
Driving towards Najac from Villefranche-de-Rouergue, you'll have to slow down on the top of the ridge to pass through the village. The old village, with its well preserved castle, ancient houses and church, is actually off to the right. The main road has a couple of shops, a restaurant called **L'Auberge** and the cave de Gayral (trade name **Gayralvin**) where you can buy local wines and the much regarded, near-lethal speciality, *la vieille prune Gayrol*.

La Fouillade

(19K S of Villefranche-de-Rouergue)
Just off the D 922, La Fouillade can be described as

> **Information:**
> Syndicat d'Initiative,
> Mairie 12270
> tel. 05 65 65 71 13

somewhere between a village and a small market town. A popular local shopping centre, it provides a good meeting place with its two bar/cafes facing the splendid Mairie. It has a couple of good local restaurants, **Le Vieux Chêne** and the **Lou Cavagnol**, and a bakery which makes the famous Najac *fouace*. (See **Food and Drink** section.)

Although you'll find the postal address for hotel restaurant **Longcol** listed as La Fouillade it is in fact much closer to Monteils along the D638.

Lunac and the Cheval du Roi

(11K E of Najac)
Apart from an uninhabited château, a charming village church, a bakery, a village shop, a post office and a bar-restaurant, Lunac's real claim to fame is its ladies' basketball team, who were not long ago the French champions! The team, **l'équipe de basket des Sérènes**, was started in 1974 and financed by the mothers of the players making foie-gras in one of the houses off the village square. The whole venture was the brainchild of the village doctor and had such good local support that Lunac's biggest most modern building is the basketball stadium. It doubles up as an indoor venue for the numerous village get-togethers.

The twelfth century church, restored in the nineteenth, is an excellent example of local building style. The semi-circular east end of the church has an attractive roof and is flanked by two rounded small chapels. Unlike many village churches, the interior restoration work undertaken is nicely in keeping with the original building.

Past Lunac on the D39, turn right and through **Lescure-Jaoul** and you will arrive at a spotheight called the **Cheval du Roi**. Situated off the road along a narrow path between fields, it offers a spellbinding view across the soft rolling countryside.

Further along this ridge road you'll find the turnings to **Bor et Bar** which will eventually bring you round hairpin bends to the tranquility of the Viaur valley.

Saint-André de Najac and Lagard-Viaur (Tarn)

(7K S of La Fouillade)
Journeying from Villefranche-de-Rouergue to Laguepie, and perhaps on to Cordes-sur-Ciel and Albi in the Tarn, you'll go through, almost bypass, the village of Saint-André de Najac. If it's time for a picnic, light lunch or breath of fresh air, then turn left off the main road sign posted towards the village centre and immediately turn left down a winding road and fierce incline which will lead you to the Viaur River valley, an old bridge crossing out of the department and a little bar-restaurant open only in Summer. Opposite, the tiny village of **Lagard-Viaur** is an extraordinary sight. The side of the river valley is so steep that it seems the houses were somehow stuck into the hillside by a giant hand.

Rieupeyroux

(23K E of Villefranche-de-Rouergue, 19K W of Baraqueville, 39K SW of Rodez)
Situated at the heart of the Ségala region, surrounded by wooded hillsides, Rieupeyroux is the main town for six neighbouring communes. It has all the modern amenities, including some newly built sporting facilities, yet it retains at its centre the charm and bustle of an old market town.

Information:
Syndicat d'Initiative,
rue de la Mairie
12240
tel.05 65 65 60 00

Local farms and forestry support Rieupeyroux's many small businesses selling seed potatoes (known throughout France for their high quality and yield) and wooden artefacts, furniture, doors and windows.

Market day:
Sunday

The town has some attractive old houses and shops around the market, but its **church of Saint-Martial** is the building of greatest architectural, historical and legendary significance. It was originally constructed in 1031 by the Benedictines of Limoges, then rebuilt in 1253, and has a most unusual series of rounded roofs, topped by a tower with a grey slate roof shaped like a witch's hat. The church is, strangely, home to a shoulder blade! It probably belonged to a large animal, but it's reputed to be that of a giant, called Samson, who so the story goes, threw one large stone from the church tower (this can be seen near the church, it now has a cross on top and has been named, unsurprisingly, **le pierre de Samson**) and hurled another large stone as far as the village of **Lunac,** some 18K away! Legend has obscured the motives for these actions.

The Centre

La Salvetat-Payralès

(34K SE of Villefranche-de-Rouergue, 11K S of Rieupeyroux)

Information:
Office de Tourisme,
Mairie 12440
tel. 05 65 81 88 43

A good deal of building has gone on since the thirteenth century, though the village has a few remaining mediaeval houses and an old gateway. The original church was demolished in the last century and replaced with a more modern one with a simple square bell tower and narrow spire. There's good home cooking to be had at the **hôtel du Commerce** and a couple of nearby **ferme-auberges,** whose details you can obtain from the *Office de Tourisme* in the place de la Poste.

Pradinas

(10K S of Rieupeyroux)
Not far from this village is the 15 hectare **Parc Animaliers de Pradinas**, open every day in July and August from 10 am to 8 pm. Here over two hundred animals are kept in wooded enclosures and there's a miniature farm where children are encouraged to meet the animals.

La Capelle-Bleys

(6K SW of Rieupeyroux, 15K SE of Villefranche-de-Rouergue, 25K W of Baraqueville)
La Capelle-Bleys is one of the many villages in Aveyron which has survived and thrived because of the addition of a new *zone artisanale et industrielle* where small workshops and light manufacturing provide a living for the inhabitants of the immediate area.

The village, once called Dousoulet, gained its independence from the neighbouring parish of Rieupeyroux in 1781 and later built up a thriving kaolin industry. A neat nineteenth century church is at the centre of this well maintained village, which also has a cafe-restaurant, **Le Douzoulet**.

On the outskirts, the new businesses, like many others in the **Baraqueville** area, concentrate on the use of wood for traditional rustic furniture. To cater for contemporary building requirements, they also make PVC-U door frames.

Sauveterre-de-Rouergue

(35K SW of Rodez, 43K SE of Villefranche-de-Rouergue)
The small bastide town of Sauveterre-de-Rouergue is

> **Market day:**
> Walnut and Chestnut Fair (weekend before All Saints' Day)

> **Information:**
> Office de Tourisme, place des Arcades
> 12800
> tel. 05 65 72 02 52
> fax. 05 65 72 02 85
> (open May to June only)

The Centre

✽
Plus beau village de France

a peaceful haven of architectural perfection in the part of the Ségala area known as 'the land of a hundred valleys' (*pays aux cent vallées*). Its central square with its eighteenth century iron cross and ancient town well is flanked by the typical bastide three or four storey houses, each with a double arched stone arcade on the ground floor, which are known locally as *gitats* or *chistats*.

The original town, built on the orders of Guillame de Mâcon, fulfilled the double function of first establishing a secular edifice to balance the religious influence of the powerful Cistercian abbey at nearby Bonnecombe and, secondly, with the later addition of ramparts, to provide security for the inhabitants of the surrounding Ségala. In spite of its fortifications, like many of the towns in Aveyron, it was occupied by the English for a time during the Hundred Years War.

There are a few shops, including one, La Licorne, which sells a wonderful collection of reproduction tapestries. The town is not over commercialised and you'll find the cafes and small restaurants charging reasonable prices. On the 'main' road to the north, opposite the town car park, is a modern but excellent restaurant and hotel called **Sénéchal,** where the chef, Michel Truchon, creates delicious and inventive dishes from fresh local produce. But check your bank balance before booking!

If you have time to visit only a few places during your stay in Aveyron, do spend a little of your time here, for quite justifiably, it has been recognised as one of the most beautiful small towns in the whole of France.

Naucelle

(35K SW of Rodez, 50K SE of Villefranche, 89K E of Millau)

Although Naucelle was convenienlty situated on the ancient Camin Roudanes road going south west to Albi and Toulouse, its early development was hindered by the proximity of the better fortified, more influential bastide town of Sauveterre-de-Rouergue. Naucelle is as old as its more famous rival but little remains of its pre-fifteenth century architecture. Even the original church, dating from 1254, was virtually rebuilt in the fifteenth century. Its more recent history, however, has benefited from the status of the N88 Rodez to Albi road and the choice of Naucelle for a railway station on the same route.

Market day:
Saturday (summer only)

Information:
Office de Tourisme, Mairie 12800 tel. 05 65 47 04 32

Naucelle now is commercially quite a busy town. Between July and August there is a market of local produce every Saturday and if you visit on the last Wednesday of each month, you'll find yourself sharing the town with four or five hundred veal calves which have been brought to the market to be sold. But for the *pièce de résistance* visit in November for the two day long *Fête des Tripoux*. *Tripoux* making in this region has its origins before the Second World War when much of the inspiration was supplied by Madame Fraysse, a lady from the town and the then acknowledged *tripoux* supremo. She taught all she knew to Charles Savy who went on to win the *'grand prix national des Meilleurs tripoux'*, awarded by the members of the *Triperie d'Or de Normandie*.

If the idea of veal calf's stomach, even mixed with a secret mixture of herbs and spices and doused in white wine, does not set your saliva running, do not be put off a visit to the retail outlet at Naucelle-Gare, called **La Naucelloise**. For here you can also buy excellent cold meats and patés made from pork, venison, wild boar and hare - all prepared to local recipes and famous throughout the area.

Dates to Note:
Fêtes des tripoux occurs on two days in November Ram market in late August

If you'd prefer to sample a plate of *tripou* before buying a jar or tin to take home, or any of a wide variety of other local dishes for that matter, try the **Hostellerie des Voyageurs** or the **Grange de la Plane** restaurants. If you'd like to stay in very special surroundings, there is the restored fortress, the **Château du Castelpers**, about 8K south of Naucelle, which has an acclaimed water front view and serves its residents with good food and wine. But it's a good idea to book first.

> **Château de Taurines**
> 13th century fortress between **Naucelle** and **Cassagnes-Begonhes**

Just 3K from the town at **Bonnefou** (towards the N88) is the twelfth century Cistercian abbey at Bonnecombe which played a major, powerful role in the Ségala region for almost six centuries. One of the many local camp sites is situated delightfully on the edge of the monks' former fishing lake.

Camjac

(3K SE of Naucelle)
This little village has, like hundreds of others, a church, a school, a few houses and the Mairie of the surrounding commune. What makes it unique is a château which has been in the Toulouse-Lautrec family for generations.

The **château du Bosc** was built in the twelfth century, largely rebuilt in the sixteenth and more recently made habitable in the nineteenth century by the grandmother of the famous painter, **Henri de Toulouse-Lautrec**. It was first opened to the public in 1954 and since then has welcomed thousands of visitors who have been fascinated to be shown round by the present owner, Henri's great niece, Madame Tapie de Celeyran. She is delighted that the château is keeping alive memories of the painter's childhood by allowing visitors to see some early sketches on the walls of the orangerie, a lounge where he would sit on the carpet and draw, and a bedroom full of toys, including a home made boat and a puppet theatre.

It is a charming venue and, unlike some of the homes of famous people, has not yet lost its soul by being turned into a commercialised tourist trap.

About 13K south of Sauveterre-de-Rouergue and a little further on from the château is the Viaduct du Viaur, an impressively constructed 220 metre long lacework of metal. The viaduct was designed in 1902 by the Parisian engineer, Bodin, who was a former student of Fiffel. It is possible to follow from here the route touristique along the **gorges du Viau**r as far as the **barrage de Jaoul**, a beauty spot in the commune of Lescure Jaoul.

Rodez

Rodez

(55K E of Villefranche-de-Rouergue, 48K NW of Millau)
The success of Rodez as a commercial and administrative city lies first in its crucial position at the centre of five surrounding areas - the **causse de Séverac**, the **Aveyron valley**, the **causse Comtal**, the **valley of Marcillac** and the **Ségala de Conques,** each of which has for centuries provided a rich supply of food, drink, building materials, metals and sources of water and energy. Secondly, high on its steep sided hilltop, it has been always easy to defend.

Evidence of the remains of the various civilisations which have inhabited the area are to be found in and around Rodez. Dolmens and menhirs abound - there are more of these in Aveyron than any other department - more than sixty monuments still exist in the commune of **Salles-la-Source**, near Rodez. From the later Celtic period discoveries of over a hundred *tertes,* burial mounds, at neighbouring

Information:
Office de Tourisme,
place Foch 12005
tel. 05 65 68 02 27
fax. 05 65 68 78 15

Floyrac have been made. The *butte* of Rodez was also a natural choice of *oppida* or fortified settlement for the Rutènes, Aveyron's Gallic ancestors. Known as *Segoduaum,* the fortified height, it was the only proper Roman city in Rouergue, with about five thousand inhabitants

The old city and some of its most splendid building were planned and built in the Middle Ages, when rivalry between church and state was such that Rodez was literally constructed as a city of two halves. **La Cité** was built for rule by the clergy and **le Bourg** for rule by secular authority in the guise of the local count - to underline the seriousness of the division, they were separated from each other for a time by a *muraille,* a high wall.

In the Church's half of the old city are the **Cathédrale Notre-Dame**, the **Place de la Cité** with its bronze statue of Archbishop Affre, killed on the barricades of Paris in 1848, and the **Espace public des Embergues** where many of the restaurants and cafés are located.

In the secular old city, the most interesting area for both shopping and historic buildings is the **Place du Bourg**, where there is also a market on Wednesday and Saturday mornings. Just off this ancient square, on the Rue St-Just, is the **Musée Fenaille**, housed in two former hotels dating from the fourteenth and sixteenth centuries. Here you'll see artefacts from prehistoric Aveyron, from the Roman period, the Middle Ages and the Renaissance with special exhibits of religious significance and illuminated manuscripts. The **Musée des Beaux-Arts** is nearby in the **Boulevard Denys Puech, place Clémenceau.**

These old parts of the city were renovated at considerable expense in 1973 when Rodez obtained government money as a *ville moyenne* (a developing area) both to conserve the ancient and expand the new. Since the Second World War, the city and its developing new industries have attracted hundreds of local young people who wanted to leave their parents' rural life and seek new opportunities, though not as far afield as Paris.

Today, Rodez has expanded way beyond the original hill settlement (though even on the hillside expansion has continued in an upward direction with numerous modern high rise buildings) and has spawned a huge area of light industrial estates and shopping complexes. The original city has 24,000 inhabitants whereas le Grand Rodez and its eight communes has more than double that number.

If you are looking for a wide variety of out of town shopping units then certainly Rodez will have more to offer than any other town in Aveyron. But for smaller, quality shops, two weekly markets, restaurants offering French and foreign cuisine, pedestrian precincts, museums, historic buildings and a cinema, the old hill city is a must. (In the Summer months arrive early to make sure of a parking space.)

As you would guess from the height of the old city, you get wonderful views. From the **Square Monteil**, you can look across to the causse du Comtal and the mountains of the Aubrac. In the **Square de Embergues**, the view is to the north and east with places and locations indicated on a Table d'Orientation. In the **Square Francoise-Fabie** (named afted the famous local poet), you can view the lower lands of the Ségala.

From which ever direction you approach Rodez, the dominant edifice is without a doubt the cathedral of **Notre Dame**, which gathers in the city and beckons to the countryside around. Even if you are not particularly interested in touring all the historic sites

The Centre

Market day:
Wednesday,
Saturday

in the city, try and make time to admire the cathedral's impressive external structure - a masterpiece of Gothic architecture - and also to view some of the exquisite internal features including sixty two choir stalls wonderfully carved by the fifteenth century craftsman, André Sulpice and a seventeenth century organ case (*buffet d'orgue*) rated as one of the most beautiful in France.

West of Rodez

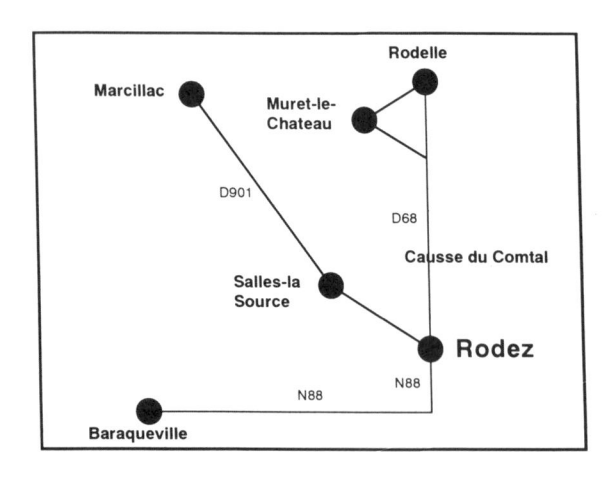

Baraqueville

(19K SW of Rodez)

This modern town has grown up around the crossroads of the D911 and the N88 from Rodez to Albi. It has hotels, a reasonable choice of small shops and half a dozen places to eat.

Informatiom:
Syndicat d'Initiative,
place du Marche
12160   tel. 05 65
69 10 78

It is a convenient stopping place for food or a night's sleep on a longer journey, especially if you don't want to go into the city of Rodez or deviate from your route. Equally it would be a suitable centre for exploring the area, with the River Aveyron to the north, the lakes of Pareloup and Pont-de-Salars to the east and the *bastide* towns of Aveyron to the west all within easy driving distance.

Market day:
Sunday
(summer only)

Salles-la-Source

(10K N of Rodez on the D901 Rodez/Conques road)
This stunning village, constucted on three levels on a hillside at the edge of the **Causse Comtal**, once boasted five châteaux and three churches built by the Counts of Rodez - now only two of each remain. In mediaeval times, the village's name reflected these aristocratic connections, as it was then known as Salles- Comtaux. Its more modern name refers to the spring water which flows through and under Salles-la-Source as a stream cascading down a twenty metre drop and is very spectacular after heavy rain.

In the central section of the village, which is called **Saint-Lament,** are numerous caves in the cliffside. If caves interest you, you can visit the largest in the area which is about 8K further north near Solsac, called the **grotte de Bouche-Rolland**.

You may notice on a map of the area that one of the major cross country footpaths, known as **Grande Routes** (abbreviated as **GR**), passes by Salles-la-Source and onwards in a northerly direction past Marcillac -Vallon. This is the **GR62** which leads from Rodez to Conques where it becomes the **GR65,** winding east and south east to Estaing on the River Lot, then, as the **GR6-65,** up into the high Aubrac.

Marcillac – vineyards and neighbouring villages

Information:
Syndicat d'Initiative,
Mairie 12330
tel. 05 65 71 72 25

(16K NNW of Rodez)
The whole valley area south of Marcillac is devoted to the cultivation of vines and the production of excellent local wines. Its sheltered situation means that it enjoys a warm microclimate. In the boulangeries and patisseries of the region the sunshine is celebrated in the intricate creation of large, circular flat pastries called *Soleils de Marcillac*. They may only take fifteen minutes to cook, but it must take a good half an hour to cut and twist the radiating rays which form the final ingenious pattern.

Marcillac itself, apart from a few shops, restaurants and bars and a fourteenth century church with octagonal bell tower, is not a very exciting town to visit. Far more interesting are the little grey or red stone-built villages to the south. If you fancy tasting the liquid products of the region, and it is to be recommended, then caves run by individual producers can be found in the villages of **Valady, Goutrens, Mouret, Combret** (which are near **Naviale), St Austremoine, Monteil, Mernac** and **Lumagnes** (which are near **Salles-la-Source**) and **Bruéjouls** (which is near **Clarivaux**).

Two films by Georges Rouquier, *Farrebique* (1945) and *Biquefarre* (1984), which won top prizes at the Rome and Venice film festivals, each celebrate rural life throughout the year near the village of **Goutrens.** His family still runs the farm after which the first film was named. Another family business just outside the village is the **domaine di Cros**, thirteen hectares of quality wine production run by M. Teulier some of which is exported to the UK.

Rodelle

(16K N of Rodez)
At this point on the Dourdou, the hillsides of the **Causse de Lanhac** generally slope quite gently down to the river. The tiny village of Rodelle, however, is perched on an odd rocky outcrop in a picturesque setting, a natural choice of site for the counts of Rodez to build a fortified settlement. They constructed the castle at one end of the promontory and the church at the other.

Close by, you'll find the **Grottes des Meule** and, way up above the village, the **Trois Rochers** from which you can get an excellent view of the causse on one side and the river valley on the other.

In the village there's the **auberge du Roc**, and you may wish to visit the **Fermiers de Fijaguet** where a local cows' milk cheese, a *tome* called *le Rodelou*, is made.

Within a short drive there are eighteenth century castles at **Dalmayrac** and **La Gondalie**. On the way to **Cruéjouls** there are three other old villages: **Saint-Affrique-du-Causse, Ceyrac** and **Gabriac,** previously a stopping place for merchants and once renowned for its horse market.

Market day:
Sunday
Wine festival on Whit Monday

The Centre

Muret-le-Château

(18K N of Rodez, 10K E of Marcillac-Vallon)
The castle was constructed in the middle ages on the orders of the bishops of Rodez and its fifteenth century tower has been recently restored. The old church of **Saint Vincent** was largely rebuilt in the eighteenth century though the original retable (altar back) and font remain.

This is a good centre for walking and exploring the small **Causse de Lanhac**. Horseriding is also available in the vicinity. The Auberge de Château serves good local food and wine.

East of Rodez

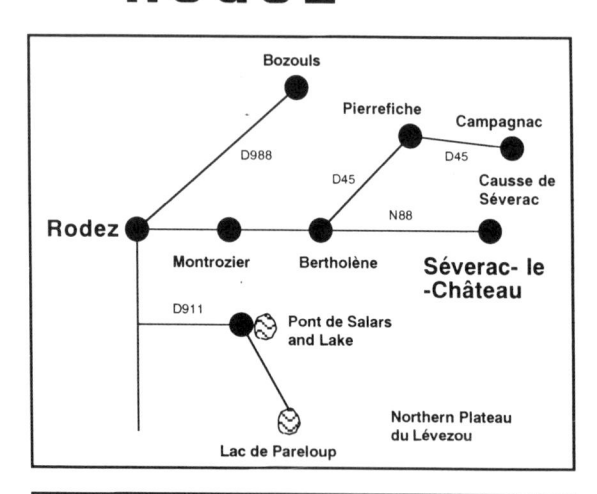

Bouzouls

Market day:
Thursday

Information:
Office de Tourisme, place de la Mairie
tel. 05 65 44 92 20

(20K NE of Rodez on the D988 Rodez/Espalion road)
This charming small town was built on and around a breathtaking natural phenomenon known as the **Trou de Bouzouls** (the hole of Bouzouls) which is now signposted as an archaeological site. The oldest part of the town is still known as **Château,** even though the thirteenth century fortress built by the counts of Rodez has long since disappeared.

Montrozier

(20K NE of Rodez off the N88)
To the north of Montrozier is the end of the **Causse du Comtal**. To the South, across the river is the **Forêt des Palanges** which marks the beginning of the **plateau de Lévezou**. The commune includes this village and **Gages** and, with its proximity to Rodez, has been an area of more recent building. The old parts of both villages have ancient castles and Gages has a fifteenth century church. In Montrozier is an archaeological museum open from May to October.

Bertholène

(12K E of Rodez on the N88)
A little further along the N88 is Bertholène. This village has an old quarter with narrow streets, a little square, a fountain and a nineteenth century church, as well as some newer development with small industries. There is also a hotel-restaurant, **Bancarel**.

The most beautiful building in the vicinity is the old castle of **Bourines** which displays a fine collection of square and rounded towers of differing heights and sizes. (The castle can be visited between 15th July and 31st August only.)

12K east is **Gaillac d'Aveyron**, a pretty little village with pleasant walks and lovely views of the river. **Laissac,** for local shopping, is to the south west.

Séverac-le-Château

(46K E of Rodez)
Geographically, the town lies in a depression

> **Market day:**
> Wednesday

surrounded by the Causse de Séverac and the plateau du Lévezou, though it is itself constructed up the side of a small isolated hill. The huge ruins of the **Château de Séverac** dominate the scene. Now the property of the commune, the site is open to the public.

As you walk up to the castle ruins from the **place de la Fontaine** and through the old town, you'll see a variety of ages of houses, the oldest dating from the eleventh century. Many more recent buildings were constructed at the turn of the century when the town was home to hundreds of railway workers after the opening of the Rodez - Millau line in 1880.

The Centre

The Causse de Séverac & the Serre Valley

> **Market day:**
> Saint-Saturnin-de-Lenne
> 4th Friday of month

North of Séverac-le-Chateau and the Aveyron valley rises the Causse de Séverac, which extends as far as the valley of the Serre. Flowing westwards, the Serre joins the Aveyron about 10K east of Rodez. The eastern limit of the causse is the department's boundary line, which also separates it from the Causse de Sauveterre.

Campagnac

(13K N of Séverac-le-Château)
The area around this village has been inhabited for over a thousand years. Dolmens and Roman remains

are testimony to the existence of settlements from earlier eras.

The ancient village houses are built of an attractive light coloured local stone. The pretty village church was completely rebuilt in the nineteenth century, but blends in well with the fortified manor house, the **Château de Beaufort**, which was begun in the fourteenth century.

2K south of the village, near the hamlet of **Canac**, is the source of the Serre. This is a wonderful area for horseriding and country walks at an altitude of between 800 and 950 metres.

Downstream, near **Saint-Saturnin-de-Lenne**, is the hamlet of **Roques-Valzergues**, where a little museum has been established, and below that at **Saint-Martin-de-Lenne**, with its three little stone bridges, is where the Serre begins to widen out.

A little to the east of Campagnac, before you come to the village of **Saint-Urbain**, is the cliffside edge of the the causse overlooking the valley of the Lot, near **Saint-Laurent-d'Olt**.

Pierrefiche-d'Olt

(33K WNW of Rodez)
This little village is in a verdant stretch of land between the Serre and the Lot, which is only 4K to the north. Indeed, an underground stream and aqueduct have only been relatively recently discovered which appear to connect the two.

Close by is the **Grange de Galinières** which was once owned by the monks of the abbey of Bonneval who had a reputation in the locality for the excellence of their farming.

The Serre is crossed for the last time by two bridges at **Coussergues,** one very old and too narrow for vehicles, and one built in the nineteenth century. After this the Serre joins the Aveyron.

The Northern Plateau du Lévezou

The plateau du Levezou, rather like Dartmoor in south west England, is a very sparsely populated area of land with high rocky outcrops, peat bogs and frequent mists. Huge lakes have been created in the west and north west by the electricity company, EDF, who have constructed enormous barrages across the Viaur and Vioulou rivers.

Vezins-de-Lévezou

(8K SW of Séverac-le-Château)

Information:
Office de Tourisme, de Monts du Levezou 12150
tel. 05 65 61 80 52

One of the most impressive views in Aveyron is from the **Puech del Pal**, the highest point on the plateau de Lévezou (1155 metres) not far from Vezins-de-Lévezou. From here the vista stretches to the Causse du Larzac in the south and the Monts d'Aubrac in the north. The source of the Viaur is nearby.

Equally pleasing to the eye is the village itself with its *lauze* roofed houses surrounding the superb fifteenth centruy castle. In July and August, one of the rooms at the chateau is open to the public for an art exhibition. There's a perfect spot for picnics in the park near the lake or there are two eating places to choose from, the **restaurant Conde** or **La Clam**.

About 8K to the south, there is a spot height near **Saint-Laurent-de-Lévezou** and **Saint-Léons**, called **Mont Seigne**, which is 1128 metres high and offers a splendid view. This is a peaty area and is famous for its wild orchids.

Pont-de-Salars and the Lakes

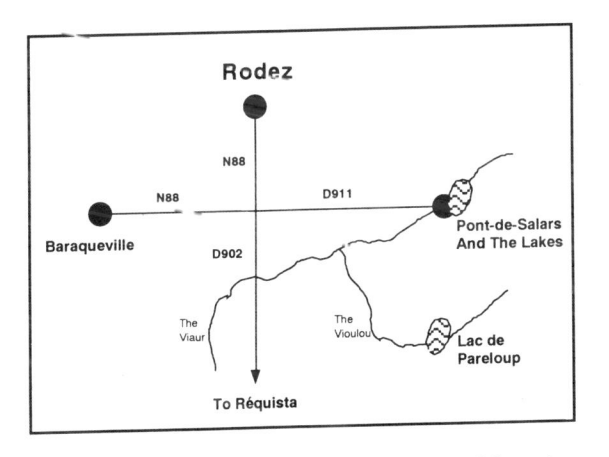

There are some delightful villages in a five kilometre radius of the lake. To the south, **Canet-de-Salars** has four campsites and a restaurant, **Les Arcades**. **Prades-de-Salar** also has a restaurant, **Liautard-Combettes**. And eastwards, there are restaurants at **Arques** and **Segur**, two villages with pretty surrounding and buildings dating from the Middle Ages. To the north, **Le Vibal** is a place for local craftsmanship - there's a wood turner, J-L Courtial, whose workshop is open weekdays and Saturdays

Market day:
Pont-de-Salars Wednesday (summer only)

from two in the afternoon in July and August, and the **Maison Creative du Vibal** which has exhibitions of local work and is open from three in the afternoon.

The obvious main attractions in this area are the lakes and the recreational facilities they provide. The **Lac de Pont-de-Salars** (190 hectares) to the north offers fishing, watersports, plus facilities for sunbathing and swimming. The water from the Viaur flows into the lake at the north eastern corner and is controlled by barrages constructed by the electricity company, EDF, in the 1950s.

The little town of **Pont-de-Salars** benefits from the huge influx of tourists into the area in the summer months. Like **Le Vibal**, it offers an outlet for local craftsmen who exhibit and sell their wares and are only too pleased to demonstrate their skills to visitors.

> Information:
> Pont-de-Salars
> Office de Tourisme,
> avenue de Rodez
> 12290
> tel. 05 65 46 82 46

Salles-Curan

(11K S of Pont-de-Salars)
South of the Lac de Pont-de-Salars is the **Lac de Pareloup** which takes its water from the Vioulou. *(Pareloup* translates roughly as 'watch out for the wolves' - a warning at one time, perhaps, to be taken seriously.) To the east of the lake lies Salles-Curan, a historic little town whose population almost quadruples in summer when holiday makers arrive for the sunshine, the watersports and the natural beauty of the area. Many of the old houses and shops have been bought as second homes, some are hired out as *gîtes,* but the most popular places to stay are the excellent campsites both here and 6 kilometres to the north near **Canet-de-Salars**.

> Market Day:
> Canet-de-Salars
> Thurday
> (summer only)

> Information:
> Syndicat d'Initiative,
> Canet-de-Salars,
> Mairie
> tel. 05 65 46 84 04

Hotels, restaurants & hotel-restaurants of the Centre

- some suggestions -

Hotels/Hotel-restaurants (* denotes Hotel Restaurant)	Restaurants
BALAGUIER D'OLT 12260	La Grange (05 65 64 63 20)
BASTIDE L'EVEQUE (La) 12200 Souyri* (05 65 29 93 00)	
BELCASTEL 12390 du Vieux Pont* (05 65 64 52 29)	Le Couderc (05 65 64 52 26)
BERTHOLENE 12310 Bancarel* (05 65 69 62 10)	
BOZOULS 12340 Le Belvedere* (05 65 44 92 66)	
La Rotonde (05 65 44 92 27)	
LA FOUILLADE 12270 Longcol (05 65 29 63 36)	Le Vieux Chene (05 65 29 63 36)
MARCILLAC-VALLON 12330 Relais de Marcillac* (05 65 71 75 57)	Le Mansois (05 65 71 84 87)
MARTIEL 12200	La Caselle (05 65 29 42 79)

The Centre

The Centre

Hotels/Hotel-Restaurants	Restaurants
MONTBAZENS 12220 du Levant* (05 65 80 60 24)	Ginestet (05 65 80 40 98)
MONTEILS 12200 Le Clos Gourmand* (05 65 29 63 15)	Miguel (05 65 29 62 61)
MURET LE CHATEAU 12330 Auberge du Chateau* (05 65 74 92 62)	
NAJAC 12270 Belle Rive* (05 65 29 73 90)	Il Cappello (05 65 29 70 26)
L'Oustal del Barry* (05 65 29 74 32)	L'Auberge de Cornaille (05 65 29 71 39)
NAUCELLE 12800 Des Voyageurs (05 65 47 01 34)	La Grange de la Plane (05 65 47 06 99)
Chateau de Castelpers 12K S on D997 (05 65 69 22 61)	
PONT-DE-SALARS 12290 Les Tilleuls* (05 65 46 82 02)	
Des Voyageurs* <u>Logis de France</u> (05 65 46 82 08)	
RIEUPEYROUX 12240 Du Commerce* <u>Logis de France</u> (05 65 65 53 06)	
Chez Pascal* <u>Logis de France</u> (05 65 65 51 13)	

Hotels/Hotel-Restaurants	Restaurants
de la Poste* Logis de France (05 65 65 52 06) **RODEZ 12000** Bastide* 12850 3K on the D988 to Espalion (05 65 67 08 15) Biney 7 boulevard Gambetta (05 65 68 01 24) Concorde* 12850 rue Beteille (05 65 68 31 61) Hostellerie de Fontagnes* 12850 3K north on the D901 (05 65 77 76 00) Tour Maje 12850 boulevard Gally (05 65 68 34 68) **SAUVETERNE-DE-ROUERGUE 12800** La Grappe d'Or* (05 65 72 00 62) Le Senechal* (05 65 71 29 00) **SAVIGNAC 12200** de la Glebe* (05 65 45 47 39) **SEVERAC-LE-CHATEAU 12150** du Commerce* (05 65 71 61 04) des Causses* (05 65 71 60 15) Moderne et Terminus* (05 65 47 64 10)	Le Chapon place de la Cite (05 65 42 53 61) Le Saint-Amans rue de la Madeleine (05 65 68 03 18) La Taverne rue de l'Embergue (05 65 42 14 51) Relais des Sources (05 65 71 61 60)

Hotels/Hotel-Restaurants	**Restaurants**
Faubourg* (05 65 47 62 46)	
du Midi* <u>Logis de France</u> (05 65 70 26 20)	
VEZINS-DE-LEVEZOU 12780	Conde (05 65 61 80 16)
VILLEFRANCHE-DE-ROUERGUE 12200 Le Relais de Farrou* <u>Logis de France</u> (4K from centre) (05 65 45 18 11)	Assiette Gourmande pl. Andre Lescure (05 65 45 25 95)
Lagarrigue* <u>Logis de France</u> place Benard-Lhez (05 65 45 01 12)	Cafe du Globe 1 pl. Republique (05 65 45 23 19)
L'Universe* <u>Logis de France</u> place Republique (05 65 45 15 63)	
VILLENEUVE 12260 de la Poste* (05 65 81 62 13)	L'Oree du Bois (05 65 81 65 77)

Moulin on the Sérène

Camping

BELCASTEL
Camping (Le Bourg)
(05 65 64 49 50)

CAMPAGNAC
Camping de la Sagne
(05 65 47 58 57)

LA FOUILLADE
Camping Municipal
(05 65 65 76 90)

MARCILLAC-VALLON
Camping Municipal
(05 65 71 74 96)

MOSTUEJOULS
Camping de l'Aubigue
(05 65 62 63 67)

International Camping des Gorges du Tarn
(05 65 62 62 94)

NAUCELLE
Camping Caravaning du Lac de Bonnefon
(05 65 47 00 67)

PONT-DE-SALARS/CANET DE SALARS
Camping du Soleil Levant
(05 65 46 03 65)

Camping les Terrasses du Lac
(05 65 46 88 18)

Camping de Retenue Paraloup
(05 65 46 33 26)

RIEUPEYROUX
Camping du Lac
(05 65 65 60 42)

RODEZ
Camping Caravaning Municipal
(05 65 67 09 52)

ST-JEAN-DE-BRUEL
Camping la Claparede
(05 65 62 23 41)

The Centre

The SOUTH

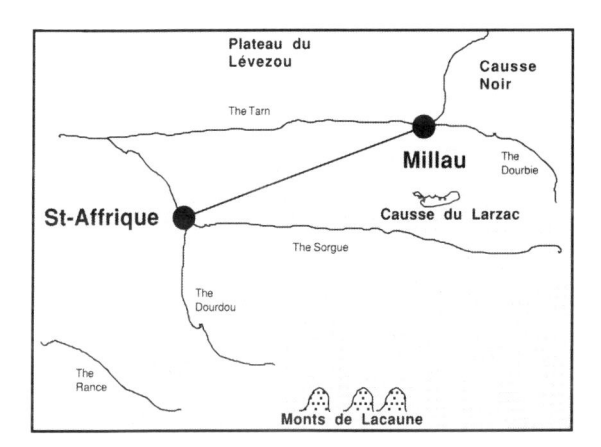

In this section

Millau
The Causse du Larzac and the 'Circuit du Larzac Templier et Hospitalier'
The Causse Noir and River Gorges
The Tarn Valley (West of Millau)
The Réquista Area
Plateau du Lévezou (North West of Millau)
North and East of Saint-Affrique
West of Saint-Affrique
South and South East of Saint-Affrique - Hotel and Camping Suggestions

The secrets of the South are unlocked by a look at a road map of the department. The multi-veined red roads linking the towns of central Aveyron narrow down to two main arteries in the South. The new A75 runs from Millau south to the Mediterranean, the older and smaller D999 crosses the width of the department to Albi in neighbouring Tarn.

> **There are over 2,000 species of wild flowers to be found in the department.**

Apart from Millau and St-Affrique there are no large centres of population. In some parts of the area sheep outnumber people, though there was a time in the 1970s when over a hundred sheep farmers were all seen together. The French government had designs on their land for military manouevres but the sight of the farmers, their tractors and some token sheep in the middle of Paris clearly influenced the eventual decision to abandon the idea.

There are places where you might feel you were the only living creature apart, perhaps, from the odd vulture flying ominously overhead. These, and many other varieties of birds, are protected by the **Parc Natural Régional des Grands Causses**, whose guardianship also extends to more than two thousand species of wild flowers, some of which on the highest land are classed as Alpine plants.

Most of the villages are in the river valleys - the Tarn, the Dourdou, the Sorgue, the Dourbie and the Rance. Some were built by the Templars who were given tracts of land in Larzac. Vast areas, however, are too rocky, too blasted by fierce winds, too long under snow and ice in the winter to be fit for human habitation. These are known as the **Grands Causses**.

Even though they are arid and inhospitable, the causses have a splendour, a magnificence and a mystery of their own. Here the geology dominates. Enormous movements in the earth's crust have created cliffs and canyons, deserted plateaus and valleys like oases in the barren landscape. Fissures and different strata of rocks conceal a vast network of underground streams and, in places, huge subterranean caverns hide secret stores of stalactites and stalagmites.

Some of these natural caves were used to store wines once produced over a wide area before the vines were decimated by phylloxera. Currently, the caves of Roquefort continue to house the maturing cheeses at a constant low temperature surrounded by a cold mist created by moisture escaping through minute fissures in the rock walls.

The weather too has played its part, with ice, wind and water eroding the soil to leave exposed rocks and stones. In the **Causse Noir**, some of the unnatural sculptures loom out of the early morning mists and haunt the evening shadows like huge mythic creatures. On a site known as **Montpellier-le-Vieux** the vast rocky formations, once surrounded by an almost impenetrable forest, were believed in the past to be the ruins of an evil city, frequented by the devil himself. Now, the whole area is a popular tourist attraction.

Between the Tarn and the Rance rivers, west and south of **Saint-Affrique**, is a gentler, lower lying region criss-crossed with scores of minor tributary streams. Some of the land, especially in the valley around **Belmont-sur-Rance**, is fertile and productive, but close to the most southerly border of Aveyron are the foothills of the high **Monts de Lacaune** in the adjoining **Parc du Haut Languedoc**.

The lakes of Aveyron (natural and man-made) cover 3,500 hectares.

The South

Millau

Historic Centre

(66K SE of Rodez)

Unlike Rodez, the capital of the department, perched on top of a steep sided hill, Millau, the *sous-préfécture*, lies in the sweep of a valley basin surrounded by higher ground at the confluence of the Tarn and Dourdou rivers. Both cities have a Roman past, though Millau's fame was more widespread because of the production at nearby **Graufesenque** (1K south) of vast amounts of pottery which were exported to the far reaches of the Roman Empire. Between the years 10 BC and 150 AD over five hundred potters at any one time created millions of red coloured vases in what must have been akin to a modern production line. From enormous kilns 7 metres high, roughly 40,000 vases would emerge from each firing. Intact examples of the work have been found in Pompeii, most of which are decorated with a distinctive swirling pattern of long-stalked leaves and flowers.

> **Market day:** Wednesday, Friday

The most recent reason for Millau being known worldwide was the glove-making industry whose history you can discover in the **Maison de la Peau et du Gant** (the leather and glove museum). The **Musée de Millau**, situated in the seventeenth century **Hotel Pégayrolles**, has excellent exhibits from prehistoric fossils to a marine reptile 180 million years old, also a fine collection of utensils, weapons, jewellery, pottery and old dolls. It also houses, inscribed on a lead plaque, the oldest and longest example of ancient Gallic text (so far discovered in France) in the form of a prayer to a dead druidess.

Undoubtedly, the most picturesque part of old Millau

Millau basin

A view from Roquefort

Causse du Larzac

- Saint-Affrique
- Abandoned farm
- Templars' route to Sainte Eulalie
- Red earth of the Rouergue

is the **place du Maréchal-Foch**, with its stone arcades dating from the twelfth century, fountain and the last remaining stone from an ancient pillory inscribed *Gara qué faras enant que comences* - 'Think about what you are going to do before you do it'.

In one of the shopping streets, **la rue Droite**, you'll come to the **Beffroi**, a splendid gothic square based tower, begun in the eleventh century and finished off in the seventeenth, with a high octagonal section. From the top of this 42 metre high edifice (which was used as a prison three hundred years ago) there's a wonderful view across the town.

> **Information:**
> Office de Tourisme,
> avenue Alfred-Merle
> tel. 05 65 60 02 42
> fax. 05 65 61 36 08

Other old buildings of appeal are the **Château de Sambucy** on the boulevard de l'Ayrolle, the **église Saint-Martin** between the place Emma-Calvé and the place du Voultre, and the **église Notre-Dame-de-l'Espinasse** off the place du Maréchal-Foch.

This is certainly a town worth spending time in for sightseeing, shopping and dining. There are numerous restaurants offering a variety of menus, and you will notice that many are serving what is called a *trenel*. Try it, especially if it's cooked in a white wine and tomato sauce. It's delicious! Afterwards ask what it's traditionally made from!

Millau is an excellent centre for exploring the ancient Templar sites, the river valleys of the Tarn and the Dourbie and the fascinating wild **Causse du Larzac** and **Causse Noir**. As well as a wide choice of hotels, there are numerous campsites, some private, some municipal, including two four star sites - **Camping Les Rivages** and **Camping Municipal de Millau-Plage**. It's an exceptional area for a real range of activities and enjoyments, such as walking, cycling, wildlife, panoramic views, dramatic geology, charming little villages and unspoilt, peaceful countryside.

The Causse du Larzac

(and the Circuit du Larzac Templier et Hospitalier)

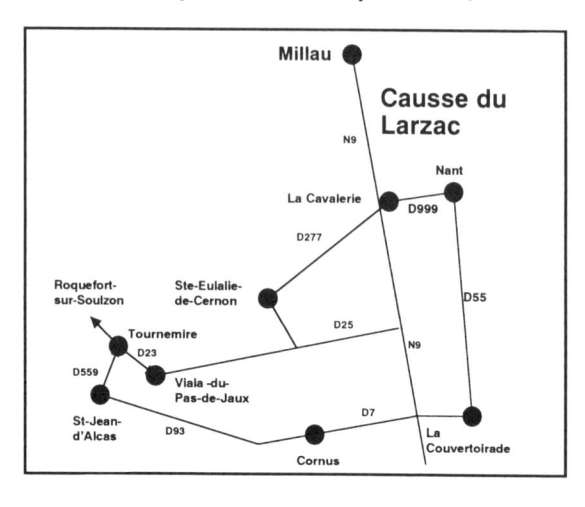

In the early days of motoring, the roads up to the **Causse du Larzac** were notorious for breakdowns - mostly from overheated radiators as the cars fought to cope with the long, tortuous climbs. Even now comparisons with the Causse du Larzac and a fortress continue aptly to be made, especially in the winter months when near blizzard conditions exist making driving hazardous and walking impossible. Even during the rest of the year the weather conditions can be frequently extreme - dramatic storms can hit in autumn with strong, cold northerly or very wet westerly winds; in summer there can be long periods of drought; and even in spring, when botanists enjoy the impressive variety of wild flowers, there can be late frosts and some very cold nights.

This 1000 square kilometre region of Southern Aveyron is home to thousands of sheep, but largely uninhabited by people apart from a few small hamlets and isolated farms. From the high plateaux there are some spectacular panoramic views across the plains, verdant basins and valleys. It was in these lower areas that the Templars and Hospitaliers created five command posts which provided well fortified stopping places for the pilgrims passing through the region on the journeys to and from Santiago de Compostella. Two of these command posts lie to the east of the A75 and three of them to the left.

> **A well signposted *Circuit du Larzac Templier and Hospitalier* provides the visitor with an excellent route to follow which takes in all five villages (sites of former command posts) and passes through some lovely countryside.**

La Couvertoirade

Starting at the most south easterly point of the circuit, La Couvertoirade possesses some excellent examples of twelfth to fifteenth century architecture. The earliest buildings date from 1159 when the Templars were given the village by the Viscount of Millau. Later fortifications were added by the Hospitaliers in the fifteenth century. Details of the history, should you be interested, can be obtained from an audio-visual display and small museum in the **hôtel de la Scipione**. The village is also home to several artists and craftsmen whose work is on display and for sale.

Saint-Jean-d'Alcas & Cornus

Continue the circuit west, across the A75 towards Saint-Jean-d'Alcas, and you'll arrive at the village of

✳

Plus beau village de France

Market day:
Sunday

The South

> **Information:**
> Syndicat d'Initiatve,
> Cornus, Mairie
> 12540
> tel. 05 65 99 38 47

Cornus which was at one time a haven for protestants, indeed it still possesses a Catholic church and a Protestant 'temple'. Saint-Jean-D'Alcas, another fortified village, was presented to the Hospitaliers in the fifteenth century, a generous gift by the Abbess of a neighbouring Cistercian abbey. It is surrounded by enormous walls and defended by four towers. Inside the town, two parallel streets of almost identical houses are reminiscent of monks' cells and maybe a reflection of the rigours of the Cistercian life style. Certainly the town is in sharp geometric contrast to the usual haphazard urban developments in the Middle Ages.

Le Viala-du-Pas-de-Jaux

Seven winding kilometres further and you come to Le Viala-du-Pas-de-Jaux given to the Templars in the twelfth century. This too was taken over by the Hospitaliers who added a large square tower which housed a cave, kitchen and two store rooms. Water for animals was stored in the four *lavognes* outside the town - these are man-made ponds like large stone basins, unique to the causse area. Nearby at **L'Oustalou de la Fadarellas** is a dolmen whose 'table' is 4.5 metres long and at **Armalières** there is a natural cave used at one time for maturing cheese.

Sainte-Eulalie-de-Cernon

Drive a further 10K and you'll come to Sainte-Eulalie-de-Cernon, a little village of considerable charm and tranquility which also began as a Templar command post in the twelfth century, indeed this was their capital in Larzac and their most prestigious town in the whole of the French Midi region. The Hospitaliers of the order of St Jean of Jerusalem took over the running of the fortification in the fifteenth century when, with local assistance, they continued to improve the defences by adding ramparts, towers and gateways. From June to September, guided tours of Sainte-Eulalie-de-Cernon are offered from 10 - 12 am and 2 - 7 pm.

Close by is the **Pic de Congouille** (912 metres) which commands panoramic views of the causse. Or if you want to stay in the area a little longer for the walking, there is a good route suggested by the local Federation Francais de la Randonnée Pedestre (the equivalent of the UK Ramblers Association), No. 44 in their 'Guide to Aveyron Midi-Pyrénées'.

La Cavalerie

The final stopping place on the circuit is La Cavalerie, back over the A75. La Cavalerie is less well conserved than the other villages but still has impressive buildings and fortifications from the Middle Ages when it was the main *village des Hospitaliers* on the ancient north/south roadway to the Mediterranean ports.

Unsurprisingly, this whole area has been much utilised by makers of historical films over many years, since little new building has taken place. Both the rural and the man-made cohere to make this a location hunter's dream with its big landscapes, the ancient stone blocks, tree clad undulations and the geometry of stone towers. Simple, romantic, historical, it is a place for big dramas on an eternal stage.

Nant

(13K E of La Cavalerie, 19K N of La Couvertoirade)
Nant and Saint-Jean-du-Bruel are the first two small towns in Aveyron near the eastern border on the

River Dourbie, which snakes its way north west to Millau. In fact Nant is at the confluence of the Dourbie and a small 8K tributary called the Durzon.

> **Information:**
> Syndicat d'Initiative
> tel. 05 65 62 12 88

In the tenth century, the area around Nant was developed both agriculturally and spiritually by the Benedictines and it was soon being talked about as the 'garden of Rouergue'. Local specialities are still produced and sold on the region's farms and smallholdings - herbs, aromatic vinegars, honeys, cheeses and even flower based wines. At **Saint-Sauveur** (just off the D991 between Nant and Saint-Véran) you can select from over forty varieties of jams and, unusually, English-style chutneys at **La Passion des Fruits**. In the restaurants you'll find locally caught *écrevisses* (crayfish) served in a variety of sauces and styles.

If you'd like to stay here, there are a couple of hotels and half a dozen campsites in the town and surrounding countryside.

One of the spectacular locations in the commune is the tiny village of **Canobre,** a few kilometres north of Nant itself on the D991, which perches precariously on the rocky cliff overhanging the river valley. Like most of its neighbouring hamlets, it has a twelfth century church and ancient houses in varying states of repair.

Saint-Jean-du-Bruel

(4K E of Nant)
This little town on the River Dourbie has some well maintained old houses, a small château and two historic bridges. During the Religious Wars, Saint-Jean-du-Bruel was a protestant stronghold whereas Nant its near neighbour, with its Benedictine history, remained catholic.

> **Market day:**
> Thursday

Its current reputation could not be more peaceful - it is a celebrated area for fly-fishing, especially for trout. It's also noted for its excellent local pâtés and terrines. The **hôtel Midi** has been well known for its cuisine and hospitality since the middle of the last century.

Information:
Syndicat d'Initiative, 32 Grand Rue 12230 tel. 05 65 62 23 64

The Causse Noir &River Gorges

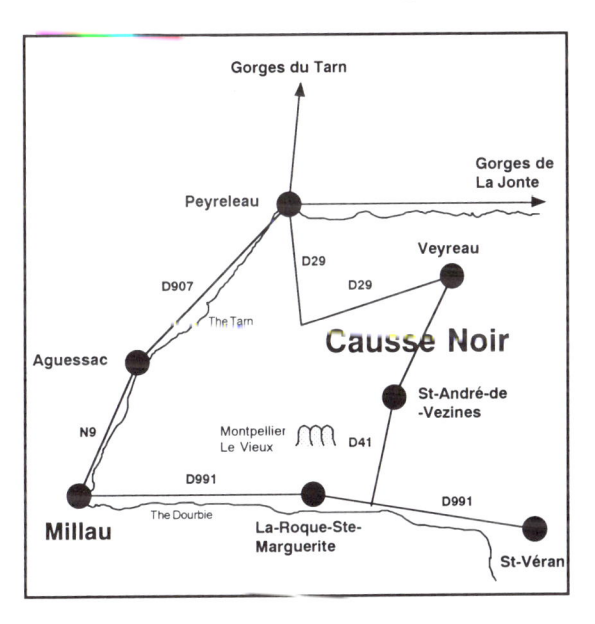

The first high plateau of the **Causse Noir** rises north east of Millau between the **gorges de la Dourbie** and the River Tarn. The second, larger half rises east to the Aveyron border towards the Cevennes.

There are three spectacular drives all starting from **Millau** on the D9, then proceeding along the D907 (which follows the Tarn valley) as far as **Peyreleau**. The first continues up the same road into the next department and into the magnificent **gorges du Tarn**. The second goes east from Peyreleau along the Aveyron border and the **gorges de la Jonte**. Finally, a circular route cuts across the causse from Peyreleau to **La Roque-Sainte-Marguerite** and back along the **gorges de la Dourbie** to Millau.

If you're staying a few days in the Millau area, its possible to explore all these, combined, perhaps, with a walk along some of the **Grand Route 62** and **62a** which cross the **Causse Noir**.

Along the first common 28K of the three routes you will travel through the following seven villages

Paulhe

This first little village has traditional old houses with grey *lauze* roofs and a sixteenth century church.

Aguessac

At the crossroads of the D9 and the **route des gorge du Tarn** (D 907) lies Auguessac. The old heart of the village has narrow streets and ancient houses. It also has some new buildings and a Palaeontological Museum. The area around the village is famous for its four varieties of cherry, some of which are conserved in the *eau de vie* and called *Escaras*. (*Escaras* is the name in occitaine given to the ladder used to reach the cherries.)

Compeyre

The village sits on a hillside overlooking the valley. In the early era of Tarn wine making, Compeyre was known for a time as the 'wine bank', because the local wine was kept in the village caves. Each year there was what was called in the local language a *tasto vin* where all the neighbours were invited for a meal and to sample the latest vintage.

La Cresse

This a pretty village is situated in the valley bottom with a steep hillside behind. Nearby there are the ruins of a twelfth century chateau and its replacement 12K to the north.

Rivière-sur-Tarn

Rivière-sur-Tarn and the **vallée du Bourg** have been immortalised, in his autobiography, by the English writer Robin Cook, who first came to the area over twenty years ago. Its other claim to fame is that the early proprietors of the local vineyards changed their allegiance from Compeyre in revolt against the somewhat restrictive practices of the *cave* owners of the village.

Mostuéjouls

Within the commune of Mostuéjouls, there are a twelfth century church at **Champs** and a castle and church at **St Marcellin**. There is an attractively sited restaurant at the nearby **hôtel de la Muse**. The whole area is very poular with campers. The commune has sprouted a dozen or more campsites of varying sizo and quality. The two largest, both three star, are the **International Camping des Gorges** and **Camping les Prades**.

Peyreleau

At one time Peyreleau was the thriving main village in the canton, but now it relies on more seasonal trade from visitors to the Causse Noir and the gorge du Tarn. It has some well preserved fifteenth century houses, and a rather magnificent modern church with rounded towers and an ancient square tower which is the last remains of a castle-fort.

The Causse Noir

The causse is *noir*, not because of any black coloured rock, but because of the dark ancient pine forests. It is the smallest of the Grands Causses (200 square kilometres) but certainly one to explore, mainly for its strange rock formations - the result of erosion by wind and water. The causse is crossed by four D roads and a lot of tracks. The major footpath, the **Grande Route 62** starts from Millau and explores the south of the causse, its side-shoot the **Grande Route 62a** veers off to the north east.

By car to reach the most spectacular of the rock formations, turn south from Peyreleau on to the D29, then onto the D110 for a short distance. You will arrive at **Montpellier-le-Vieux**, not a town, but what was mistaken for the eerie, evil ruins of one by early travellers. It is in fact a most extraordinary collection of huge eroded rocks, first officially discovered in 1883, then explored and mapped by E-A Martel in 1885, who gave names to the various sections and individual 'rock-sculptures'.

At the entrance, a parking area is provided. A circular route is now worked out for visitors which takes about an hour and a half to complete on foot. It starts from the *Cenotaph* and goes on to the *donjon*, *le Dourminal* which offers an excellent view of the whole area. Another spotheight (830 metres) a little further on is known as *les ramparts* and beyond that again is the impressive *Porte de Mycenes*. From here the pathway turns back up *le nez de Cyrano de Bergerac* to the *Grotte de Baume Obscure* where Martel discovered the bones of a prehistoric bear. Then it's back past *la tête de Harlequin* to the car park. This all sounds like some awful prehistoric Disney Park. It's perhaps better to go with none of the names in mind and be utterly spellbound by the sheer majesty and strange ancient beauty of the place.

There are really only four main centres of habitation on the Causse Noir:

1. Veyreau

In the north east corner is Veyreau, near the **gorges de la Jonte**. Above it is a viewing point near St Michel's hermitage where there are the ruins of an old chapel. From here you can see across the **Causse Méjean** and the **Cirque de Madasse** - another strange outcrop of 'rock sculptures'. In the village you can buy several varieties of award winning honey from Joel Blanc and eat at the **auberge de Cadenas**, whose owners also offer horseriding.

2. Saint-André-de-Vezines

Just south of Veyreau is one of Aveyron's many menhirs at **Vessac** on the D41. To the south west is the hamlet of **Saint-Jean-des-Balmes** with its eleventh century church and fifteenth century chapel.

This village is right in the middle of the Causse Noir. It has a fine example of a lavognes - a man-made basin for collecting rainwater. To the south is the site of **Roc Altes** not far from **Montpellier-le-Vieux**.

3. La Roque-Sainte-Marguerite

Market day:
Tuesday (summer only)

La Roque-Sainte-Marguerite is built on the hillside, overlooked by the seventeenth century chateau, whose chapel, restored in the eighteenth century is now the village church. If you just want to visit **Montpellier-le-Vieux** on the Causse Noir then from Millau it's a quicker drive along the **gorges du Tarn** road, theD991.

4. Saint-Véran

In the south east corner of the Causse Noir, Saint-Véran will be found near the **Ravin de St-Véran** on the Dourbie. It's a pretty little village whose houses have the old *lauze* roofs. About 7K south, continuing on the D991, is the hamlet of whose houses and church are perched on top of a sheer rocky cliff and are over shadowed by some huge eroded rock formations.

The Tarn Valley (West of Millau)

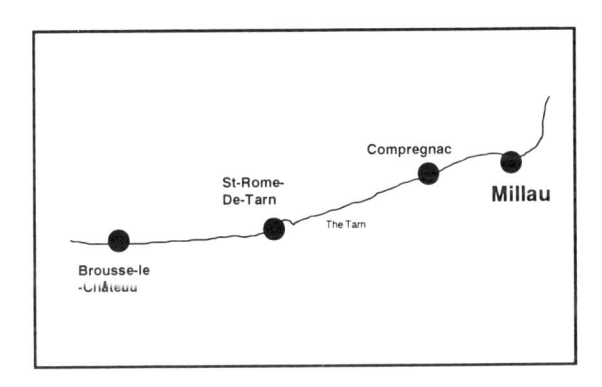

Some roads follow the river valley all the way from Millau west and south west across Aveyron to the border just beyond **Brousse-le-Château**. (The Tarn then winds its way to Albi and Gaillac.)

Compregnac

(9K W of Millau)
The village has a little auberge, charming houses, a nineteenth century church and a chateau. To reach it, you pass the hamlet of Peyre, built into the hillside.

Saint-Rome-de-Tarn

(23K W of Millau)
This is the first town of any size you come across after Millau. It has a variety of styles and ages of houses (the earliest date from the eleventh century) in its picturesque streets and is a charming place to

> **Information:**
> Syndicat d'Initiative, place Terral 12490
> tel. 05 65 62 50 89

visit for a meal or as a centre to stay longer for walking sightseeing or canoeing. From here it's worth driving to the **Plateau du Lévezou** to the north of the Templar villages of the **Causse du Larzac** to the south east.

Nearer to Saint-Rome itself there is a wonderful stretch of the River Tarn eastwards for about 20K which has **Les Raspes**, the **lac de Pinet**, the **lac du Truel**, the **lac de Saint-Amans**, a couple of little riverside hamlets and opportunities for various watersports. You may also enjoy walking around the commune of **Saint Victor et Melvie** with its ancient hamlets, streams and dolmens.

Brousse-le-Château

✳
Plus beau village de France

> **Market day:**
> Tuesday (summer only)

(25K WSW of St-Rome-de-Tarn)
Brousse-le-Château was constructed on an easily defended natural site above the Tarn. The twelfth century castle and the houses of the village have benefited from the initiative, hard work and capital supplied by the locality. You can now visit this early model of military architecture with guided tours mornings and afternoons in the summer months. If you want details in advance contact the **Foyer Rural de Brousse** (05 65 69 40 15).

Brousse le Château

The Réquista Area

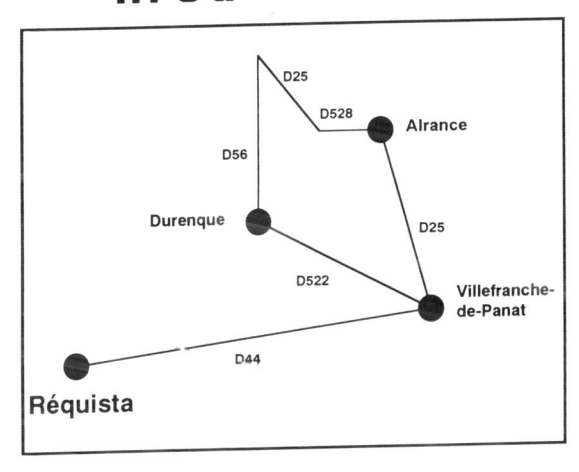

Between Réquista and Baraqueville to the north is some fairly low lying agricultural land crossed by the Viaur River, its tributary the Ceor and countless small streams. The land to the east of the Réquista / Rodez road gradually climbs to the higher Lévezou and the lakes of east-central Aveyron. A few towns and villages in this region are worthy of note.

Réquista

(51K S of Rodez)
A look at the road map will easily illustrate that Réquista is strategically placed about 50K from Albi, Rodez and Saint-Affrique - for centuries an obvious commercial crossroads. Even its name denotes financial success, for it comes from two local words *ric estar* meaning rich place. Originally it was created as a bastide in 1292 by Henri II, Count of Rodez, but

Market day:
Saturday

it was burnt to the ground by the English when they occupied the area during the Hundred Years War. The only house to survive was owned by three young, beautiful sisters who were being courted by English officers. The town suffered again (by French hands this time) during the religious wars and was further damaged by fire in 1701.

Information:
Syndicat d'initaitive
place Charles de
Gaulle 12170
tel. 05 65 46 11 79

Consequently, Réquista is not a town to visit if you like historic buildings. Its more recent history has seen the return of commercial success, some industry is based on farming - milk for the Société des caves de Roquefort from local sheep and the sale of animals - but numerous light engineering companies and furniture makers have also established themselves here. In the vicinity, it is also a popular centre for shopping.

Villefranche-de-Panat

(19K NE of Réquista)

Market day:
Thursday, Sunday

Information:
Syndicat d'Initiative,
Mairie 12430
tel. 05 65 46 52 04

The town lies to the south of the **Lac de Villefranche-de-Panat** and has become a very popular spot for holidays. It has the advantage of being a historic town in an excellent geographical location. The tourist industry has expanded successfully thanks to some astute planning and building in the commune. As well as offering water sports, fishing and lovely lakeside locations, there are a village de vacance and municipal campsite to amply accommodate visitors. There's also a good lakeside restaurant at **Hostellerie du Lac**. It even boasts one of the biggest megaliths in Aveyron - a huge dolmen near the **ruisseau de Betaille**.

Durenque

(9K WNW of Villefranche-de-Panat)

The high land of the Lévezou extends to a plateau around Durenque and Alrance known as **Le Lagast**. Its highest point (927 metres) is shown on the map as **Pyramide du Lagast** and is just to the north of Durenque. The village surrounds its old church which was in danger of falling into complete ruin until an enterprising stone mason bought the ruined village castle early in the nineteenth century and used the stones to rebuild the church tower.

Information:
Syndicat d'Initiative
tel. 05 65 46 41 39

A most charming little museum is to be found in the **moulin de Roupeyrac**, birthplace of the French poet Francois-Fabie. The building's interior is one typical of the region in the nineteenth century, with authentic furniture and cook-ware of the time.

Alrance

(5K N of Villefranche-de-Panat)
The village has somewhat revived since EDF built a generating station in the commune. It is a convenient place to stop for a walk up to the **Tour de Peyrebune** where there are wonderful views across the Lagast and the lake at Villefranche-de-Panat. If you build up an appetite, good food can be had at the village restaurant **Le Chaudron**.

Cassagnes-Bégonhès

(25K N of Réquista)
This ancient little town is 25K north of Requista on the Rodez road in the Ceor valley. Its history goes back to the thirteenth century when it was first under the protection of the king, then the counts of Rodez. In some ways it was rather like a bastide, its inhabitants had the same freedoms and privileges and its huge church tower is reminiscent of that in the central square of the bastide town of Villefranche-de-Rouerguo.

Market day:
Monday (3rd week in month, summer only), Friday

The town suffered badly during the religious wars when the Protestants burnt and destroyed nearly three quarters of the old buildings, but enough remains to make it an interesting place to visit.

The small aerodrome outside the town on the **plateau de Cancart** was the first to be built by a rural commune.

On the third Monday of the month there is a sale of veal calves and on those days you'll be advised to arrive early if you want lunch, especially at the popular local restaurant **chez Eugene Vernhes**.

Plateau du Lévezou

(North West of Millau)

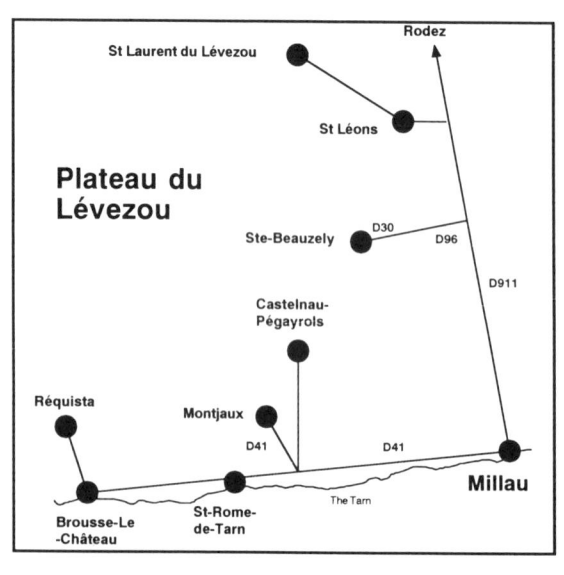

The plateau du Lévezou lies within the boundary of the **Parc Naturel Régional des Grands Causses** and is a good one hundred and fifty metres higher than either the Causse Noir or the Causse du Larzac. Five villages lie in a line at the feet of the sharply rising, uninhabited plateau which is crossed by three minor roads, the slighlty larger D993 and an awesome stretch of the public footpath from Millau, the **Grande Route 62.**

Montjaux

(16K W of Millau)
The most southerly of the five villages, Montjaux, lies half way between the Tarn River and the plateau. The original village with its twelfth century church and collection of old houses, some with lovely gothic and renaissance detail, is charming. The newer part was built along the road from Rodez to Saint Affrique and has a comparatively recent sixteenth century chateau. (The ruins of the first chateau, built in the thirteenth century, lie outside the village.) The area is good for walking and you'll come across numerous dolmens and *cazelles* (tiny dry stone walled shepherds' huts) - relics of previous civilisations.

Castelnau-Pégayrolles

(15K WNW of Millau)
This small village is in the extraordinary position of having two eleventh century churches! The smaller, the **église de Notre Dame**, is situated at the cemetery and houses some seventeen century frescos. The larger, the **église St Michel**, is architecturally superb, built by the monks of the abbaye de Saint-Victor de Marseille who added a priory shortly after which was restored in the fifteenth century. The castle of Castelnau dates from the

twelfth century - one of the oldest fortresses in Rouergue, it dominates the surrounding countryside. It functions both as landmark and reminder of feudal times gone by.

Saint-Beauzely

(12K NW of Millau)

The village of Saint-Beauzely lies another 5K north, just off the main Rodez / Millau road, the D 911. It's an historic little town with a thirteenth century castle and a fine collection of old houses, surrounded by the sixteenth century ramparts. The castle was originally owned by the Gaujal family who later gave it to a religious order. It is now owned by the commune and houses the *syndicat d'initiative*. Nearby is the lovely priory of **Comberoumal** founded in the twelfth century on land donated by the count of Rodez. You may be interested in attending the concert of sacred music held there each August.

> Information:
> Office de Tourisme,
> Le Chateau 12620
> tel. 05 65 62 03 90

Saint-Léons

(21K NNW of Millau)

Saint-Léons was a religious wanderer from Aquitaine who, attracted by the location's natural charm and beauty, settled here in the fifth century and built a monastery. Little remains of the original edifice- a few bits of wall and Leon's tomb. The fifteenth century chateau, however, is still very much in existence and is open to tourists as much sought after *chambres d'hôtes*. The castle grounds and an exhibition of paintings are open to the public in the afternoons in July and August. There's also a museum open in the summer months and some good homemade food at the **relais du Bois du Four**.

Saint-Laurent-du-Lévezou

(22K NNW of Millau)
The little village of Saint-Laurent-du-Lévezou is built on the side of the **Mont Seigne** and has little but a church and a small cafe. If you'd like to climb up to the summit (1128 metres) you'll have a fantastic view of the Aubrac as well as appreciating why the site was once chosen for a prehistoric fort.

North and East of Saint-Affrique

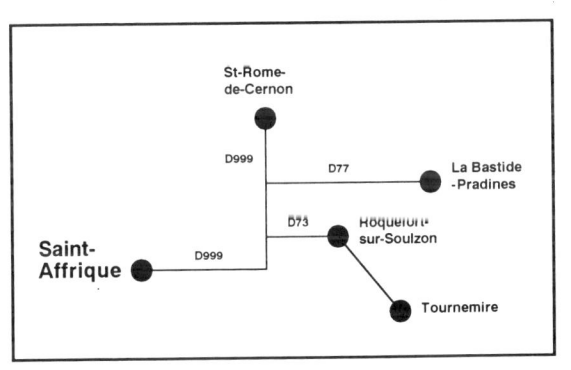

```
                St-Rome-
                de-Cernon
                   ●
       D999        |       D77        La Bastide
         ──────────┼──────────●       -Pradines
                   |
                  D73   Roquefort
                   ●────sur-Soulzon
Saint-             |
Affrique   D999    |
   ●───────────────┘    ●
                        Tournemire
```

Saint-Affrique

(26K SW of Millau)
Saint-Affrique is a large town of almost 8,000 inhabitants on the River Sorgues, just before it joins the Dourdou. It's surrounded by hills and, in a somewhat small imitation of Rome, is known as *la ville aux sept collines*. In the past, it was a very

Market day:
Tuesday, Thursday

successful textile town, but this industry dwindled during the industrial revolution. Now its biggest employer is Mazarin which offers works to about nine hundred people. Other smaller firms dealing in electronics and electrical components are thriving here too. There are also a large abbatoir and several food processing companies.

> **Information:**
> Office de Tourisme,
> boulevard de Verdun
> 12400
> tel. 05 65 99 09 05

The town's history goes back to the sixth century when Saint Affricain, bishop of Comingues, established an early church, having been chased out of Saint Bertrand-de-Comingues by the Visigoths. A small settlement grew up around the church and his tomb which named itself after him.

The River Sorgues is crossed by three bridges in Saint-Affrique - **le pont Vieux** with its three arches and hump back dates from the fourteenth century; the **pont Neuf** was built in 1792 and the **pont de Centenaire** constructed in1889. It is a very popular place for fishing the abundant supply of trout, tench and carp.

If you come into Saint-Affrique on the D999, you'll find three parking areas near the river and one on the right as you come into the town from the Millau direction.

The town is an excellent centre for shopping, eating out and making day trips. With its river and park it's also a pleasant place to wander and have a picnic. You can guarantee authentic regional food at the Decuq family's **hôtel Moderne**, for in 1969 Francois Decuq published *Cent et une recettes de cuisine aveyronaise* - a book which has become a bible for local cooks.

Within easy reach of Saint-Affrique is the **rocher de Caylus** which, due to erosion. looks just like an ancient fortress. It's likely it was the site of a castle-fort built by the count of Caylus in the fourteenth century and destroyed by the count of Toulouse. From the *table d'orientation* at **Puech Bourillon**, there is a splendid view of the town below, the river and the surrounding countryside. If you are interested in dolmens, you can search out thirty or so around Saint-Affrique, the most famous being the **Dolmen de Tiergue**, about 7K out of the town on the D993.

Roquefort

(9K NE of St Affrique)
The town of Roquefort is rather dull and grey, but its setting is spectacular and its cheese production absolutely fascinating.

As you drive from Saint-Affrique towards Roquefort, you'll see the imposing sweep of the cliffs of Combalou. Within the unique structure of the rock and caves lies the secret of the success of Roquefort cheese. Millions of tiny fissures in the rock allow cold damp air to permeate the caves. This means that the cheese can be kept at a temperature around 8 degrees centigrade and a 95% humidity. Over 150,000 people visit the caves each year to be shown around the whole production process.

Information:
Office de Tourisme,
Mairie 12250
tel. 05 65 59 93 19
mid-June to
mid-September

You have the choice of two companies to visit. **Les Caves Société** are open for tours between 9 - 11 am and 2 - 5 pm. The **Caves Alric** where Roquefort Papillon is made are open from 8.30 - 12 am and 2 - 6 pm in winter and 10 am - 7 pm in summer.

Above the village are ruins of an eleventh century chapel and a *table d'orientation* with views to Larzac and the plateau of Lévezou.

About 20,000 tonnes of Roquefort cheese are produced each year for worldwide consumption.

Tournemire

(11K NE of St Affrique)
The history of Tournemire is the history of the rise and fall of the rural railway. The first train on its way to Millau stopped here in 1874. As a consequence of the station being the junction of the Béziers - Paris and the Albi - Vigan lines, the place blossomed for more than fifty years. Then, slowly, the service was reduced for both passengers and freight and Tournemire was left as a minor stopping point on the line.

The geography of the village's setting is quite stunning. Set in the **Cirque de Tournemire**, it has its own vast fortifications, the precipitous cliffs of Larzac. A subterranian stream emerges from the rocks and joins the waters of the Soulzon. Close by is the **rocher de Castelviel** (the ruins of a lost village), the **grottes de Matarel**, which once were used for maturing cheese, and the **grottes du Brias**.

La Bastide-Pradines

(16K NE of St Affrique)
For some reason this ancient village is not included in the region's prescribed 'Circuit du Larzac Templier et Hospitalier'. Maybe because it is built on a rocky spur slightly to the west of the main body of the causse. Anyway, it does have a huge thirteenth century building called the Castel or Granieyras - an ancient fortified granary built by the Templiers de St-Jean de Jerusalem and then placed under the authority of the Hospitaliers. Strategically it was a command post on the old road from Narbonne to Rodez.

Saint-Rome-de-Cernon

(9K NE of St Affrique)
The village grew up around a crossroads where the route from Nant met the Millau - Saint-Affrique road. The original settlement was on a hillside with its thirteenth century castle, now in ruins, on the top. A more modern part has been built on the right bank of the Cernon connected to the old village by a nineteenth century bridge.

West of Saint-Affrique

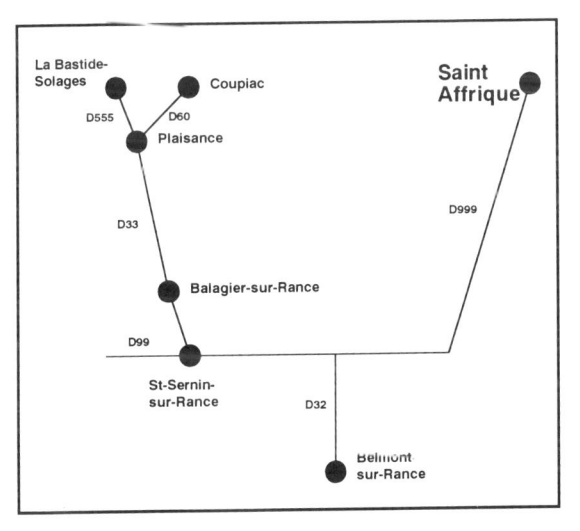

This area is crossed by two rivers, the Dourdou and the Rance, and has two colours of rock, red in the **Rougier de Camarès et Belmont** and grey in the more southerly **Monts de Lacaune**. Both of the rivers are good for fishing, especially for trout, but not after heavy rain when the water of the Dourdou turns into a red torrent from which it usually takes a couple of days to settle down.

Coupiac

(12K N of St-Sernin-sur-Rance)
This is the largest settlement close to Aveyron's western border. The village has a reputation for furniture making and once played a leading role in the surrounding canton before the boundaries were changed and Coupiac came under the wings of Saint-Sernin-sur-Rance to the south. Plans are afoot to restore completely the fourteenth century castle which is now owned by the commune. If you arrive at mealtime, you'll find good, simple food at **l'hostellerie Renaissance**.

> Information:
> Syndicat d'Initiative,
> Mairie,
> au pays des 7 Vallons
> 12250
> tel. 05 65 99 72 56

There are some pretty locations by the streams and little rivers in this area, such as the the Mousse and the Gos. **Saint-Exupère** is a very picturesque spot.

Plaisance

(10K NW of St-Sernin-sur-Rance)
The buildings in this delightful village are on both sides of the River Rance. Most are on a small hill with a drop on one side to the river. On the other side, the **Château royal de Curvalle** was built in the thirteenth century, the advantageous site having caught the eye of the Count of Toulouse. After its seventeenth century owner, the Baron of Senegas, was banished for various crimes, such as assassinations and the destruction of chapels, an order was issued for his property to be rased to the ground.

Apart from the village church, the most enticing building is a beautiful house of fourteenth to seventeenth century construction with lovely furniture and garden. The smells are good too, for within its walls is the **Les Magnolias**, home of some inventive, well presented dishes of local produce.

La Bastide-Solages

(3K NW of Plaisance)
This little hamlet lost its original chateau in the last century when its new owners, obviously minus a sense of history, saw no attraction in the old building. Fortunately, they didn't have any influence on the natural surroundings. There are some lovely nearby stretches of the Rance (which for about 15K is also the Aveyron boundary) and just west of the village at Saint-Pierre it joins the Tarn which flows on to Albi.

Saint-Sernin-sur-Rance

(32K WSW of St Affrique)
In spite of losing most of its old castle (the last remaining tower has been incorporated into the village church), Saint-Sernin has retained its mediaeval charm in its narrow streets and ancient houses with timber frames and over-hanging top storeys. The village, built on a hillside overlooking the Rance, offers the visitor not only a sense of history but also some quiet country walks in the wooded hillsides and by the river. There are also a swimming pool and an excellent restaurant at the **hôtel Carayon.**

Information:
Syndicat d'Initiative,
Mairie 12380
tel. 05 65 99 62 84

Belmont-sur-Rance

(23K SW of St Affrique)
This village, 10K from the southern border of Aveyron, is hidden away in hilly terrain just above the

River Rance. The houses are snuggled up around the imposing building of the **Collégiale**, the church of the monastery. In fact, they nestle so closely in such narrow streets that to get a good view of the Collégiale it's best to walk up to the top of the village and look down.

Belmont has tried very hard to update its image to attract tourists and improve the lifestyle of its inhabitants. It is aware of its historic attractions (lovely timbered houses houses, religious buildings, a Gothic bridge) but also offers the modern in the form of a swimming pool, an aerodrome and a *piste de karting*.

> **Market day**:
> Sunday

> **Information:**
> Syndicat d'Initiative,
> Mairie 12370
> tel. 05 65 99 93 66
> fax. 05 65 99 98 06

South & South East of Saint-Affrique

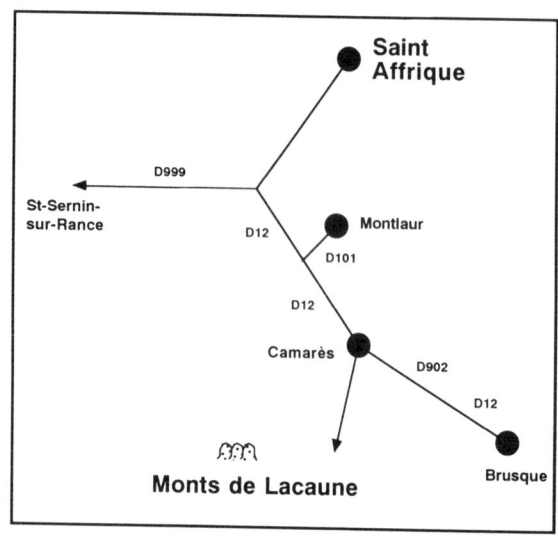

Only **Camarès,** on the Dourdou, has a population of over one thousand. **Brusque**, further up river to the south east, has about four hundred, **Montlaur** just over five hundred and all the other villages (and there are not many of them) have fewer than a hundred inhabitants. Some are really no more than hamlets.

Indeed, if it were not for the Templars creating their fortified villages towards the Causse du Larzac, there would be very little man-made of note in the whole of this southern part of Aveyron. Having said that, however, it is an amazing area in terms of changing countryside - mountains and river valleys, thriving farmland and stark, wild aridity, greys and reds of the rocks and a unique variety of flowers and birdlife.

Montlaur

(12K S of St Affrique)
The village of Montlaur sits quietly by the River Dourdou, probably very much as it did before the Hundred Years War between the French and the English which resulted in a considerable amount of damage to property. Rebuilding and renovation has taken place over the centuries, most recently the nineteenth century bridge had to be repaired after the Dourdou flooded. Keen anglers from all over southern Aveyron visit the river and its numerous streams, maybe dropping in to refresh themselves at one of the village's three hotel-restaurants.

Camarès

(10K SSE of Montlaur)
Old Camarès is in a beautiful hilly wooded area above the river, with **la Cloque**, an industrial area along the banks. From the buildings around the castle, it is obvious that the place had a fairly prosperous history. Several of the houses along the

Market day:
4th Wed. of month

> **Information:**
> Syndicat d'Initiative,
> 29 Grand-Rue
> 12360
> tel. 05 65 49 53 76

narrow streets have ornate windows and doors, homes of the once successful merchants and middle class of Camarès. The current light industries continue to enable the town to thrive. There are two hotel-restaurants, the **Pont Vieux** and **hôtel Monteils**.

Brusque

(10K SE of Camarès)
Since the First World War, the commune gradually saw its population leaving to find work in larger towns. It's only recently that the houses have been bought as holiday homes which start opening up in March when the fishing season begins. Brusque's tourist industry has also gradually developed since the opening of the **village de vacances de Ceras**.

Certainly, it is an absolutely lovely area of natural attractions. The village houses are built along narrow streets reaching part of the way up a steep hill which rises from the winding river valley and is topped by the inevitable ruins of a castle.

Students of English history will be interested in the nearby **Ermitage de Saint-Thomas** where the ill-fated Archbishop of Canterbury, Thomas a Becket, spent some time hidden away in religious contemplation in the **fôret de Brusque**.

Hotels, restaurants & hotel-restaurants of the South

- some suggestions -

Hotels/Hotel-restaurants	Restaurants
(* denotes Hotel Restaurant)	
ALRANCE 12430	Le Chaudron (05 65 46 50 85)
AGUESSAC 12520 Le Rascalat* Logis de France (05 65 59 80 43)	
CAMARES 12360 du Pont Vieux* Logis de France (05 65 99 59 50)	
CASSAGNES-BEGONHES 12120	chez Eugen Vernhes (05 65 46 70 08)
COUPIAC 12550 Hostellerie Renaissance* (05 65 99 78 44)	
MILLAU 12100 Cevenol Hotel rue Rajol (05 65 60 74 44)	& Pot d'Etain
International* place Tine (05 65 59 29 00)	Aub. de la Borie Blanque Route de Cahors (05 65 60 85 88)
La Capelle Occitaine place Fraternite (05 65 60 14 72)	Auberge Occitane rue Peyrollerie (05 65 60 45 54)

The South

Hotels/Hotel-Restaurants	**Restaurants**
Des Causses* Logis de France avenue Jaures (05 65 60 03 19)	La Braconne place Foch (05 65 60 30 93)
	La Mangeouire boulevard de la Capelle (05 65 60 13 16)
	La Terrasse rue St-Martin (05 65 60 74 89)
	Le Square rue St-Martin (05 65 61 26 00)
MONTLAUR 12400 L'Oustalet (05 65 99 80 26)	
MOSTUEJOULS 12720 de la Muse et du Rozier* (05 65 62 60 01)	
NANT 12230 du Commerce* (05 65 62 25 11)	Le Menestrel (05 65 62 26 88)
Le Durzon* (05 65 62 25 53)	
des Voyageurs (05 65 62 26 88)	
PLAISANCE 12550 Les Magnolias* Logis de France (05 65 99 77 34)	
SAINT-AFFRIQUE 12400 Moderne* Logis de France Avenue Pezet (05 65 49 20 44)	Palais Gourmand boulevard Tremolet (05 65 99 07 43)
Annexe les Tilleuls (05 65 99 07 24)	Auberge Occitane rue Peyrollerie (05 65 60 45 54)

Hotels/Hotel-Restaurants	Restaurants
de France 5 rue Industrie (05 65 99 00 94)	du Plo Le Plo de Moussigny (05 65 49 42 47)
ST-JEAN-DE-BRUEL 12230 du Midi* Logis de France (05 65 62 26 04)	
ST-LEONS 12780	relais du Bois du Four (05 65 61 86 17)
ST SERNIN-SUR-RANCE 12000 Carayon* Logis de France (05 65 98 19 19)	
VEYREAU 12720	l'auberge de Cadenas (05 65 61 17 99)
VILLEFRANCHE-DE-PANAT 12430 Hostellerie du lac* (05 65 46 58 07)	

River Tarn

The South

Camping

AGUESSAC
Camping Municipal
(05 65 59 84 67)

ALRANCE
Camping les Cantarelles
(05 65 46 40 35)

BELMONT-SUR-RANCE
Camping le Val Fleuri
(05 65 99 95 13)

COMPEYRE
Camping des Cerisiers
(05 65 59 87 96)

COMPREGNAC
Camping le Katalpa
(05 65 62 30 05)

MILLAU
Camping les Erables
(05 65 59 15 13)

Camping St Pal
(05 65 62 64 46)

Domaine de Pradines Camping Caravaning
(04 67 82 73 85)

NANT
Camping Val de Cantobre
(05 65 58 43 00)

RIVIERE-SUR-TARN
Camping de Peyrelade
(05 65 62 62 54)

Camping les Peupliers
(05 65 59 85 17)

ST-ROME-DU-TARN
Camping la Cascade
(05 65 62 56 59)

Camping et Gites de la Base Nautique
(05 65 58 11 06)

Glossary

Balet	Small balcony at the top of external stone steps up to the door of house on first floor.
Buron	Small building which serves as summer home for Aubrac cattle farmers in the high pastures. Cheese is also made in the burons.
Causse	A chalky plateau whose surface is dry and rocky.
Cazelle	Tiny, dry-stone walled, circular buildings - a refuge for shepherds.
Commune	A collection of small hamlets/ villages. One village heads the commune and contains the Mairie, There are just over 300 communes in Aveyron.
Department	A regional division of France. Created after the French Revolution, Aveyron roughly replaced the old area of Rouergue. Departments are all numbered according to their alphabetical order. Aveyron is 12 - a number used on car registrations and as part of the postal address.
Dolmen	A megalithic tomb with a large flat stone laid on upright ones.
EDF	The French Electricity Company which has built many barrages across rivers for the purpose of generating hydro-electric power and in some areas creating new lakes in the process .

Gitat	Covered area under stone arcades.
G.R.	Grandes Routes are signposted footpaths across France. They are marked on maps with the letters GR, plus a number (eg.GR62).
Hospitaliers	A military and religious order of knights founded in the eleventh century. They took over the Templars land and property after 1312 and fortified many of their buildings in Aveyron.
Lauze	Flat, thick oval slate.
Lavogne	A circular depression lined with stone to collect rainwater for animals.
Menhir	A tall, upright monumental stone.
Montagne	High pastures in the Aubrac, each about a hundred hectares.
Puech	A promontory, a high outcrop of rock.
Puy	Like puech, a name given to high rocky outcrops - usually the peaks of hills.
Ségala	Land where rye was grown.
Templars	A military and religious order of knights established in 1119. They were given lands near Lauzac where they built stopping places for Christian pilgrims, whom they had vowed to defend. Envy of their wealth led to their brutal elimination on the orders of the king of France, who confiscated their wealth and gave their land and property to the Hospitaliers.

Reading

J-L. Aubarbier, M. Binet et J-P Bouchard	Aimer l'Aveyron
Daniel Crozes	Vous Guide en Aveyron
Elizabeth David	French Provincial Cooking
Editions Bonneton	Aveyron
Editions Subervie	Recettes Paysanne en Aveyron
Fédération Francaise de Randonée Pédestre et le Conseil Général de l'Aveyron	Aveyron - Les Chemin de la decouvérte
Rosemary George	French Country Wines
Rex Grizell	South West France
Hachette	Guide Bleu
Henriette Guilliem	La bonne cuisine du Sud-Ouest
Bernard Houliat	Les Sentiers d'Emilie autour des Gorges de l'Aveyron
Michelin	Gorges du Tarn, Cevennes, Bas Languedoc (Guide Vert)
Michelin	Guides 1997 and 1998
Offices de Tourisme et Syndicats d'Initiatives de l'Aveyron	L'Aveyron en Randonée
Margaret Rand	The Red Wines of France
Geneviève Saurel & Michel Lombard	Au Pay de Najac
Jeanne Strang	Goose Fat and Garlic
Paul Strang	Wines of South West France
P. and J. Strang, J Shenai	Take 5000 Eggs
Anne Willan	French Regional Cooking

In me the soul of our forefathers
                              lives on
I am the stone beneath their feet
                              become erect
I am the tree in morning mist
                              become thought
I am the water over rocks
                              become language
I am the earth beneath their skin
                              become poem

> from L'AME DE L'AVEYRON
> by
> Jacques Bâtides

Index

Aguessac	**144**
Aligot	18, 22, **23**, 33
Alrance	**152**
Ambeyrac	**96**
Aubin	15, **78**
Aubrac	**61**
Auzits	**77**
Balagier-d'Olt	**96**
Balledou	**71**
Baraqueville	15, 87, **117**
Bastide	19, 20, 21
Bastide-l'Evêque, La	**101**
Bastide-Pradines, La	**161**
Bastide-Solages, La	**163**
Belcastel	**102**
Belmont-sur-Rance	15, 135, **163**
Bertholène	**122**
Bleu des Causses	21
Bonnefou-d'Aubrac	**62**
Bor et Bar	**108**
Bouillac	**80**
Bournazel	**103**
Bouzouls	15, **121**
Brommat	**56**
Brousse-Le-Chateau	**150**
Brusque	**166**
Buron	18, 24, 63, 171
Cabécou du Fel	23, 72
Camarès	15, 165, **166**
Camjac	**113**
Campagnac	15, **123**
Cantal de Thérondels	21, 22
Capdenac-Gare	14, 15, 53, **81**
Capelle-Bleys, La	**110**
Carladez, Le	52, **54**
Cassagnes-Bégonhès	15, **152**
Cassuéjouls	**59**
Castelnau-de-Mandailles	**63**
Castelnau-Péygayrolles	**155**
Cathars	11, 104
Causse de Comtal	11, 88
Causse de Lanhac	120
Causse du Larzac	125, 137, **138**
	150, 165
Causse Noir	135, 137, 138, 150
Causse Rouge	11
Cavalerie, La	**141**
Champignons	27

Château du Bosc	113
Château de Castelnau	**68**
Château de Graves	**92**
Cheval du Roi	108
Compeyre	**145**
Compolibat	**101**
Comprégnac	**149**
Confits	29, 30
Conques	15, 17, 53, **73**
Cornus	15, 26, **139**
Coupiac	**162**
Couvertoirade, La	**139**
Cransac	53, **77**
Cresse, La	**145**
Decazeville	14, 15 25, 53, **78**
Drulhe	**98**
Durenque	**152**
Enguialès	**72**
Entraygues-sur-Truyère	15, 32, 53,
	64, 71
Espalion	15, 58, **69**
Espeyrac	**72**
Estaing	15, 64, **70**
Estofinado, L'	25, 28
Flagnac	**81**
Foie gras	29, 30
Forêt de Palanges	122
Fouace	25, 76
Fouillade, La	**100**
Fritons	30
Gaillac d'Aveyron	**122**
Golhinac	**70**
Gorge de l'Aveyron	102
Gorge de la Dourbie	76, 144
Gorge de la Jonte	144
Gorge de la Truyère	65
Gorge du Dourdou	76
Gorge du Tarn	144, 148
Gorge du Viaur	141
Grande Houtes	61, 64, 101
	118, 144, 146
Graufesanque	136
Grotte de Bouche Rolland	118
Grotte de Brias	160
Grotte de Foissac	90
Grotte de la Gleio de Maou	95

Index

Grotte de Loudon	102
Grotte de Materel	160
Grotte de Meule	120
Lacalm	**58**
Lac de Castelnau	68
Lac de Couesque	57, 64
Lac de Galens	64
Lac Maury	64
Lac de Montezic	57, 64, 65
Lac de Pareloup	89, 126
Lac de Pont-de Salars	89, 126
Lac de Sarrans	56
Lac de Selves	57, 64
Lac du Truel	150
Lacroix-Barrez	56
Laguiole	15, 58, 59, **60**, 64
Laguiole (cheese)	21, 22
Laissac	15, 122
Livinhac-le-Haut	80
Loc-Dieu, Abbey of	94
Lunac	**107**, 109
Marcillac-Vallon	15, 17, **119**
Martiel	94
Millau	13, 15, 26, 134, **136**, 144
Montagne d'Aubrac	11, 18, 52, **57**, 58, 61, 63
Monteils	105
Montbazens	15, **160**
Montjaux	**155**
Montlaur	**165**
Montpellier-le-Vieux	**147**
Monts de Lacaune	135, 162
Montsalès	95
Montrozier	**122**
Mostuéjouls	**146**
Mur-de-Barrez	15, **54**, 57
Muret-le-Château	120
Najac	15, 87, **103**
Nant	**141**
Naucelles	15, **111**
Nayrac, Le	**64**
Noix	26, 27
Parc Animaliers de Pradines	110
Parc des Oiseaux	93
Parc du Haut Languedoc	135
Parc Natural Regional	
de Grands Causses	88, 134
Paulhe	**144**
Pays D'Olt	53, **65**
Peylereau	15, 26, 144, **146**
Peyrusse-le-Roc	**98**
Pierrefiche-d'Olt	**124**
Plaisance	**162**
Plateau du Lévezou	14, 88, 89, **125**, 150, **154**
Pont-de-Salars	15, **126**
Pradinas	**110**
Prévinquières	**101**
Puech des Condamines	63
Puy de Barry	63
Puy de Compech	68
Réquista	15, **151**
Rieupeyroux	15, **108**
River Alzou	87
River Argence	57
River Aveyron	87, 91, 101-105, 114, 123
River Dourbie	134, 137, 142, 148
River Dourdou	52, 74, 77, 134, 136, 162
River Lot	11, 17, 52
River Rance	134, 162, 163
River Serre	123, 124
River Sorgue	134, 158
River Tarn	11, 134, 136, 144, 145, 148, 149, 150, 155, 163
River Truyère	11, 17, 52, 57, 58
River Viaur	11, 14, 87, 89, 125, 126
River Vioulou	89
Rivière-sur-Tarn	**145**
Rodelle	**120**
Rodez	14, 15, 87, 88, **114**
Romans	11, 13, 91, 115, 136
Roque-Sainte-Marguerite, La	144, 148
Roquefort (cheese)	21, 29
Roquefort-sur-Soulzon	**135**, 159
Rougiers de Camarès et Belmont	162
Rougiers de Marcillac	53
Rutènes	11, 13,90,115
Saint-Affrique	15, 134, 136, 158
Saint-Amans-des-Cots	15, **64**
Saint-André-de-Najac	**108**
Saint-Andre (cheese)	23

Index

Saint-André-de-Vezins	**148**
Saint-Beauzely	15, **156**
Saint-Chély-d'Aubrac	15, 61, **62**
Saint-Côme-d'Olt	**68**
Saint-Cyprien-sur-Dourdou	**76**
Saint-Geniez-d'Olt	**67**
Saint-Jean-d'Alcas	**139**
Saint-Jean-de-Bruel	**142**
Saint-Laurent-d'Olt	53, **66**
Saint-Laurent-du-Lévezou	**157**
Saint-Léons	**156**
Saint-Rome-de-Cernon	**161**
Saint-Rome-du-Tarn	15, **149**
Saint-Sernin-sur-Rance	15, **163**
Saint-Symphorien-de-Thénières	**65**
Saint-Véran	**148**
Sainte-Croix	**94**
Sainte-Eulalie-de-Cernon	**140**
Sainte-Eulalie-d'Olt	**67**
Sainte-Geneviève-sur-Argence	15, 57, 64
Salles-Curran	**140**
Salles-la-Source	114, **118**
Salvagnac-Cajarc	95
Salvetat-Peyrolès, La	15, **109**
Sanvensa	106
Sauveterre-de-Rouergue	13, 20, 87, 110
Savignac	**94**
Ségala	12, 66, 87, 88, 122
Sénergues	**72**
Série Bleue Maps	39, **40**, 87
Séverac-le-Château	15, 26, 88, **122**
Soleils de Marcillac	119
Stockfish	24, 26
Templars	11
Thérondels	**55**
Tome Fraîche	23, 24
Tournemire	160
Trénel	26
Tripoux	26
Truffes	26
Truques d'Aubrac	62
Veyreau	**147**
Vezins-de-Lévezou	15, **125**
Viaduct du Viaur	114
Viala-du-Pas-de-Jaux, Le	**140**
Villefranche-de-Panat	**152**

Villefranche-de-Rouergue	13 15, 18, 19, 20, 23, 25 26 87 **90**
Villeneuve-d'Aveyron	15, 20, **97**
Wines - Entraygues et le Fel	32, 72
Estaing	33, 70
Marcillac	31
Vins des Gorges et Côtes de Millau	34

Forthcoming Titles

- The Basque Lands

- The Catalan Pyrenees

- The River Aveyron - Its Valleys and Gorges

- The Islands of Samoa

For the latest details on further publications in the series, contact the Secret Places Website;

http://www.secret.places@btinternet.com

Or you can e-mail us with your comments and suggestions at;

secret.places@btinternet.com